W9-BYA-399

9 Secrets of Women Who Get Everything They Want

Also by Kate White

Why Good Girls Don't Get Ahead . . .

but Gutsy Girls Do

9 Secrets of Women Who Get Everything They Want

KATE WHITE

Harmony Books
New York

Copyright © 1998 by Kate White

All rights reserved. No part of this book may be reproduced
or transmitted in any form or by any means, electronic or
mechanical, including photocopying, recording, or by any
information storage and retrieval system, without permission
in writing from the publisher.

Published by Harmony Books, a division of Crown
Publishers, Inc., 201 East 50th Street, New York, New York
10022. Member of the Crown Publishing Group.

Random House, Inc. New York, Toronto, London, Sydney,
Auckland
www.randomhouse.com

HARMONY and colophon are trademarks of
Crown Publishers, Inc.

Printed in the United States of America

Design by Rhea Braunstein

Library of Congress Cataloging-in-Publication Data
White, Kate, 1950–
9 secrets of women who get everything they want / by Kate
White.—1st. ed.
1. Women—Conduct of life.   2. Success.   I. Title.
BJ1610.W525   1998
158.1'082—dc21   97–45975

ISBN 0-517-70756-X

10 9 8 7 6 5 4 3 2 1

First Edition

To my fabulous parents,
Anne and Charles,
who gave me everything
a girl could want.

CONTENTS

ACKNOWLEDGMENTS

Thank you to my wonderful editor, Shaye Areheart, who provided such great guidance and support.

9 Secrets of Women Who Get Everything They Want

BEGIN AT THE BEGINNING
The Art of Having Your Cake and Eating It, Too

Is there something you want right now in a bad, bad way? Something you've been craving but just don't know how to get? Like a one-hundred-year-old Victorian house with a wraparound porch and four fireplaces and a bookshelf-lined study? Or a really good promotion, like the one that just went to that awful woman at the other end of the hall who's two years younger than you and mispronounces the word *paradigm*? Or the chance to finally live in San Francisco? Or fifteen fewer pounds on your body? Or your kid paired up with a teacher who really believes in her? Or a wonderful guy, the type who won't give you a set of car mats for your birthday and can hear the word *marriage* in a conversation without looking like he's just been served a plate of boiled eel?

Or maybe you have a vague restlessness and sense of longing, but you're not at all sure what the longing is for.

Whether you're craving something so clear that you can almost taste it or your longing is an undefined "I-know-I-need-something-but-I-don't-know-what-it-is," I'd like to offer a few secrets that can help you get what you want.

What makes me such a big fat expert—and why in the world am I willing to share?

Over the past few years I've come to see that I'm really good at getting what I want. I have a wonderful job as the editor in chief of a magazine, a good husband, two kids, and a lovely home in Manhattan—and, so far at least, I haven't been cursed with stress acne or a peptic ulcer as punishment from the gods.

Please don't think I'm bragging. I haven't always known how to get what I want. Rather, it's a skill I had to learn. For years I was on the sidelines. You could say I was a little like Skipper, always watching Barbie have all the fun and furniture and fur-trimmed evening dresses.

I don't want to imply that I used to be a total sad sack. All through my twenties I was a hard worker with lots of enthusiasm, and I saw many of my efforts pay off for me. But despite my occasional victories, I ended up with the booby prize much of the time—and I wasn't sure what I was doing wrong. I moved to New York City right after college, which was the fulfillment of a dream I'd had since I was twelve—but I ended up living in a depressing, cockroach-infested apartment in an old tenement building, while my friends managed to snag cute digs with exposed brick walls that resembled the adorable apartment Mary Richards lived in. I soon landed a job as an editorial assistant at *Glamour* magazine, and after two years was promoted to feature writer, but then I got stuck—unable to either proceed up the ladder at *Glamour* or to find a better job elsewhere. I was living in a city bursting with smart, attractive single men, yet I always ended up with jerky guys, one of whom I had the bad judgment to marry. In other words, I sometimes got my cake, but I never managed to eat it, too.

It wasn't simply that I didn't know how to get what I wanted. Some of the time I wasn't even sure *what* I wanted or which dream I should be pursuing.

So how did I finally end up in the catbird seat? Some of my success is due to trial and error and the confidence that comes with time. But for the most part I stole all the best ideas from women who are brilliant at getting what they want.

You know exactly the kind of women I mean. The ones with fantastic jobs and fantastic boyfriends/husbands and fantastic houses—and have you ever noticed how they all seem to have fantastic haircuts, too? Those are the women I studied and copied.

The Art of Having Your Cake and Eating It, Too

Now, you've certainly noticed these women in action, and you may have assumed there was nothing you could learn from them because they seem to get everything handed to them on a silver platter—thanks to looks or money or family heritage or a remarkable sense of their own destiny. And, of course, there's some truth in that—just take

Carolyn Bessette-Kennedy. Of all the tidbits the press turned up about her after her wedding to JFK Jr., my personal favorite is the fact that, in high school, she and several friends had formed a group called the Billionaires' Wives Club. From this nugget it's absolutely clear that the woman who won JFK Jr., and has been designated a style icon for the nineties, always had this astute awareness of her potential and, ultimately, simply got what she felt she deserved. Her sense of entitlement turned her into a magnet for life's most delectable rewards. As one acquaintance said to *New York* magazine, "She knew that she possessed all these qualities to make herself kind of an 'It' girl. She knew all these talents were going to take her somewhere."

Other women get what they want because they are born with megadoses of beauty or talent or both. I still remember the first time I met a woman like this. I was a junior promotion writer at *Glamour,* a terribly dull job that consisted of writing brochures about advertisers' products. I occupied my considerable downtime by chatting with the receptionist as she hand-studded all of her boyfriend's denim clothes. One day, while I was standing at her desk, a young woman got off the elevator and asked us where she could find the model editor's office. She mentioned that she had recently arrived back in America after living for a few years in France, and that this was one of her first appointments. She was beyond pretty and absolutely glowing, with big blond hair that had a zillion split ends, but you just knew that with the right hairdresser and a deep conditioner, she would be perfect.

4

After she was hustled off to the model editor's office, I turned to the receptionist and uttered just one word: "Wow." You could tell that this woman was destined to be a star. I discovered a few weeks later that her first appointment with the editor had led to a booking for a fashion shoot and that the fashion shoot had led to a *Glamour* cover. Christie Brinkley's career was launched.

No, you can't become Carolyn Bessette-Kennedy or Christie Brinkley. But getting what you want isn't just a matter of believing you deserve to marry a billionaire or having the beauty trifecta of fab hair, fab face, and fab thighs. There are lots of women who get what they want because they work at it. They've discovered the techniques that land the big kahuna and they use them.

Sharon Stone proved that she had become a master of these techniques as she headed to the Academy Awards ceremonies in '96, the year she was nominated for her role in *Casino.* Her best friend had given her *The Little Engine That Could* because she considered it the story of the actress's life. "I think I have much less talent than I have guts," she said. "But because I kept persevering, I took the little bit of talent and made it the best it could be."

There are people who would argue that getting what you want in life isn't something that you can learn from anyone else. If you're destined to be one of the world's winners as opposed to one of its perpetual whiners, it's because you have been born with the right talents and temperament and have a big dose of self-esteem, ambition, and good judgment. But I think you can have talent and skill and not land the prizes because you go about it the wrong way. You need to learn the secrets like I did. I got them for free and I'm happy to pass them along. If there's something you really want, I guarantee they'll work for you.

My First Lesson (or How I Finally Saw the Snows of Kilimanjaro)

I have always been a shameless admirer of smart, capable women, and from the time I was about sixteen, I paid attention to their sense of style, the way they talked and walked, and the way they pulled off their magic. But for a number of years, that's all I did—*admire* them. Then finally, one day, I realized I could also imitate them. That's how, for instance, I got to be a world traveler during the years I was earning next to nothing in starter jobs in the magazine business.

All through college, I had dreams of moving to Manhattan after graduation and becoming a combination magazine editor/international adventuress. I pictured myself working hard in a glamorous job but also having lots of free time to travel to exotic locations, where I'd drink in bars with ceiling fans and sleep at night under mosquito netting. But once I saw what was in my paycheck after the government got its paws on my paltry salary, my hopes for such a lifestyle were dashed. I knew I'd be lucky to afford bus rides to Boston to see my college roommate. Plus, I learned, to my horror, that I only got two weeks of vacation time a year. Before I started at *Glamour,* I'd had this vague sense that I was still entitled to an out-of-school-for-the-summer vacation.

A month after I started working and still in a state of despair, I met a young editor on the staff named Catherine who had just come back from a safari in Kenya, where she'd eaten grilled impala and had an affair with her British safari guide. I was completely enchanted with Catherine. She was tall and thin with startlingly short hair—sort of an Amelia Earhart type—and I followed her around like a puppy dog, listening to her stories of the Serengeti and the other places to which she'd traveled. I knew she made under $20,000 in her job, so I assumed she was a rich chick—like several of the other underpaid *Glamour* editors. But it soon became clear, from several remarks she made, that she was living on her salary alone.

Finally, one day I got up my nerve to ask her about it. "You've got to tell me something," I nearly begged. "How do you take all those fabulous trips?"

"What do you mean?" she asked, smiling a Cheshire cat smile.

"How can you *afford* them? They must be so expensive."

"I have this secret strategy," she said. "It's really simple—and yet I've never met another woman who uses it. If you try it, you can go all over the world just like I do."

At this point I was nearly foaming at the mouth in excitement.

"Please, please," I pleaded.

"Well, every week I have ten dollars from my paycheck automatically deposited into my savings account. By the end of the year I have over $500 for traveling."

I almost groaned in disappointment over the pedestrianness of her "secret." Her advice was about as exciting and surprising as the directions on the back of a package of boil'n bag vegetables. But after I got over my disappointment, I decided it wouldn't hurt to try it. Financially it would mean a sacrifice. Believe it or not, ten dollars a week was a lot for me to give up—so much of my income was earmarked for rent. I made a vow to convince more guys to pay for my beers at the neighborhood watering hole.

There was another essential tip Catherine shared with me. To take exotic trips, you have to have extra time off. Most bosses, she'd discovered, would cave in if you pleaded and promised you'd work like a dog when you returned.

Within a year, I'd saved more than $500. I talked my boss into giving me three weeks off and I spent a week in San Francisco and two weeks in Hawaii on one of the most glorious adventures of my life. Over the next years, every time my salary went up, I'd arrange to have more money taken out of my paycheck (eventually, I got rid of the passbook account and had my travel funds put into CDs). I traveled alone all over the world—I went on safari to Kenya (a tribute to Catherine), explored the Mayan ruins of the Yucatán, tagged penguins in southern Argentina, jetted to London for a glorious weekend, and helped restore an archaeological site in Rarotonga, a beautiful little island in the South Pacific. And in some respects I owed it all to Catherine.

My passport to adventure wasn't all Catherine gave me. She also taught me the art of buying 7 pieces of clothing and mixing and matching them so they look like 114 outfits. Around this time another young *Glamour* editor began inviting me to her house for dinner parties, and from her I learned all sorts of tricks on how to be the perfect hostess (three of her favorite strategies: serve tons of wine, invite at least two stupendously cute guys, and allow people to congregate in your kitchen, particularly if it's small and they must be bunched together).

The more I watched and learned from these women, the more I saw that they got what they wanted because they went after it—rather than waited for it to arrive miraculously at their door after they'd wished really, really hard. *They fired their own jets.* At times it might appear that their success resulted effortlessly, that fate simply liked them better, but behind the scenes they were always working their fannies off. I read a great line by Demi Moore lately that summed it up beautifully: "I have a career, a marriage, and children and I am an independent woman. I don't have any magic. I have these things because I worked to create them."

Women like this work at it in every area of life—job, love, home. It's not that they're control freaks. They just go in there knowing that if you want things to come out a certain way, you have to *make* them come out that way. I had an amusing experience lately that showed just how much control you can exert. I was hosting a luncheon in Washington, D.C., for *Redbook* at which Elizabeth Dole was the keynote speaker. One of the little things I discovered firsthand about her—besides her beauty and charisma—was that she took charge of how she was photographed. When a photographer attempted to take her picture as she was holding a glass during the preluncheon reception, she would raise a finger to indicate that he should wait until she put the glass down. During the luncheon, she never allowed her picture to be taken while she had food in her mouth. She'd smile nicely at the photographer, raise a finger to make him stop, and then point to her cheek.

The brilliance of this strategy became clear to me when I looked at the photos later. In every shot she is poised and elegant. I, on the other hand, hadn't taken such precautions, had left everything to chance. There are pictures of me looking like I'm chewing a softball and others in which I'm slinging a glass around as if I'm at the Chi Psi cocktail party.

Of course, you can't control everything. But women who get what they want operate with a sense of percentages. As one enviable woman I know says, "I figure that there's about 15 percent of life I can't have any power over. But the other 85 percent I can. And so I always start with the attitude that I'm going to at least try."

The Secret Strategies

While having your cake and eating it, too, calls for a can-do attitude, it's not as simple as that. If it were, I'd just end here, sending you on your way with a quick "Go get 'em, baby."

As I watched women who get what they want, I began to recognize that they pursued their goals using a whole set of special strategies. It wasn't simply a matter of grabbing the bull by the horns. They chose the perfect time to approach the bull, grabbed just the right way, and were careful as they walked away. And here's the kicker. Most of these strategies, interestingly enough, are the exact opposite of the classic advice I'd always heard. Their rules bore no resemblance to the rules I'd been living by.

Over the following pages I'm going to share the strategies of these women who get what they want. They've worked for me over and over again; I know you can make them work for you. You may be surprised as you read on because, as I've said, in most cases these rules are the exact opposite of conventional wisdom. You may be initially skeptical, and it may seem awkward when you first begin to try them, but trust me, the more you use them, the more natural they'll feel.

Why is it that some women have learned them and others haven't? Some women have had good teachers. Others stumbled on the effectiveness of the strategies early, after they'd tried the conventional approach and found it lacking. It doesn't really matter. All you have to do is ask yourself: Why should they have all the fun? These methods are there for all of us to purloin and use to our advantage.

But Do I Have to Be a Pit Bull or a Prima Donna?

As I talk about women who get what they want, it's possible that some very nasty images will come to your mind: Eva Peron, Imelda Marcos, Joan Crawford, Leona Helmsley, Alexis Carrington, the little witch down the hall at work who listened to your idea for a new product and then pitched it to the boss as her own.

Certain women get what they want by using the ugliest of methods. There are several different categories of these meanies. First is the prima donna, who makes demands that so flabbergast people that they do not know how to say no. I was booked to give a speech recently at the same conference at which a well-known celebrity would be speaking, and one of the event promoters told me how uncomplicated it was making my arrangements in comparison to the celebrity's, whose list of "requirements" was four pages long. One of the items stated that her hotel room should have a fruit basket but under no circumstances should there be more than two bananas in it. You just have to wonder what happens when there are *three*.

Then there is the snake, who sneakily goes after her prey, lying a little, cheating a little, using some slimy flattery, insinuating herself into the right places. When I was in my twenties, a young woman who was a friend of a friend began asking my boyfriend and me to parties and events at her apartment. It surprised me because she didn't seem particularly interested in me. One night she invited us to an atrocious dinner party, at which my boyfriend was seated to her right and I was banished to the end of the table next to a weirdo who refused to eat any dairy products because, as he explained impatiently, "I never drink from the udder of another species." You're probably catching on faster than I did, aren't you? Two months later my boyfriend belonged to the hostess.

Last, but hardly least, is the pit bull. Her methods are far more obvious than the snake's, but she is so quick and so fierce that no one can stop her. She barges in, grabs something with her teeth, and won't let go.

What is so annoying about these women is that their methods seem to work. Most of us don't have the conscience or stomach for such behavior, and the good news is that you don't need to come even remotely close to the character traits I've just described. The tactics in this book will leave no one feeling bloodied or betrayed.

A Few Basic Warnings

Using the techniques in the following pages will get you what you want, but there are a few things you must be aware of.

• You cannot get *everything* you want *all* the time. That is just a fact of life. Even the most talented prima donnas look into their fruit baskets at times and discover that they have been given three bananas.

• There's a difference between getting what you want and getting what you want and enjoying it. We all know people who have grabbed some incredible prize—whether it's the top rung in their career or a husband with absolutely tons of money—and still they aren't happy.

Getting what you want can involve trade-offs big and little. But you shouldn't be miserable. I have focused only on women who get what they want and go to bed smiling.

• And last, but not least, as you get more and more of what you want, it will greatly irritate some people. That is a fact of life. You must learn to thicken your skin.

1

COVET THY NEIGHBOR'S THINGS

Before you can begin to get the things you want, you must first know exactly what they are. When you read profiles of or see interviews with successful women, have you ever noticed how damn sure they are of what they want? It may seem a little obnoxious, but then again, that certainty has given them the strength and determination to go after their dreams like a heat-seeking missile.

Some of us grow up with a very specific passion—a desire to be a veterinarian or an artist, to have a whole brood of kids, or to live in the mountains. Donna Hanover, television journalist, First Lady of New York City, and now actress (she played Ruth Carter Stapleton in *The People vs. Larry Flynt*), knew from the time she was in high school that she wanted to be in front of television cameras. Her school had a closed-circuit TV setup, and students involved in the speech and debate clubs did a newscast. The first time Hanover was "on-air," she felt a charge she'd never experienced before. "I thought, 'Whoa, this is for me,'" she says. "It was like I'd come home. There was a rush of adrenaline while I was doing it, the feeling of being very much in the moment."

But for many of us there's no clear, precise goal. We feel passion, but it has fuzzy outlines and we aren't sure where to go with it. I have an extraordinarily dynamic friend who bounced from one career to the next for many years knowing only that she wanted to be in charge of something. She just wasn't sure what that something should be.

You can start out absolutely sure of what you want, but end up confused by lots of outside factors. Another friend grew up wanting kids, and when she and her husband married, she assumed that one day they would have them—though there was no great rush. The years went by without them trying to conceive. They enjoyed Caribbean vacations and their new house and their evenings in nice restaurants, and finally, as she stared age thirty-five in the face, she felt the time was right and she raised the subject with her husband. His response knocked the wind out of her.

"We've built such a great life," he said. "Why would we want to upset it by having kids?"

She felt panicky. She'd assumed, mistakenly, that he'd been thinking along the same lines—let's enjoy this phase of our lives together and then, when we're ready, we'll go on to the next. Like a good partner, she now tried to see things from his perspective. They did have a special life, just the two of them, and they'd gotten awfully spoiled having lots of time for themselves and money, too. There was also the danger that if she pushed him to have a baby when he didn't want one, the marriage would suffer. Suddenly, she didn't have a clue as to what she really wanted.

And then sometimes you can want something with all your heart that is literally impossible. I grew up deliriously infatuated with the idea of working at a magazine, and even put out my own little neighborhood publication, writing all the material myself. How nice to have found my calling at the age of ten. But when I finally got a job at a magazine, I realized that I'd been mistaken about what working at a magazine would involve. I'd always thought it meant being a writer, when, in fact, most magazines are made up of editors who assign articles to freelance writers working out of home offices. Now what? If I moved up the ladder at a magazine, I wouldn't be able to write. If I became a freelance writer, I wouldn't be working at a magazine. I wasn't sure which of those two things I wanted.

Women who get what they want are good at knowing *what* they want. When they talk about what they have, they use phrases like "I'm nuts about it" and "I wouldn't trade this for anything in the world" and "I'm absolutely in love with what I'm doing." Don't be intimidated. You, too, can feel that way about something.

The Bad Feeling That Leads to Good Things

Several months ago I went to hear a talk by Helen Gurley Brown, the former editor in chief of *Cosmopolitan* magazine and now head of all the international editions of *Cosmo*. She rarely gives speeches, but this group had persuaded her to say a few words at a luncheon just after she'd retired from her job as one of the most successful and influential editors in chief in magazine publishing history. I have always admired her greatly and I was dying to hear what she'd have to say.

After the talk, I went up and said hello—we've known each other professionally for many years, ever since I went to interview her when I was twenty-nine (after I'd left *Glamour* and become a senior editor at *Family Weekly* magazine). I told her how much I'd learned from observing her. "Oh, I envy you, Kate," she said. "You're in the prime of your career."

On my walk back to the office, I thought about how gutsy she'd been to say the *E* word. Envy's a feeling nice girls don't like to experience let alone *admit* they're experiencing.

And yet one of the discoveries I've made about women who get what they want is that they aren't ashamed to let themselves feel envy. They see something another woman has and they think, "That's wonderful. I want it, too."

Don't get me wrong. Envy isn't a pretty feeling. The reason they say "green with envy" is that the first rush is followed by the sensation you'd get if there was a terrible backup of bile in your stomach. Plus, envy often isn't content to just sit there making you sick and miserable. When we're vulnerable and impatient, it can lead to bad behavior. You may become snippy or ugly toward the person you feel envious of or you may even turn to sabotage. Because of the out-of-control potential of such feelings, we generally do our best to keep envy at bay, to ignore it, deny it, suppress it.

But if envy were all bad, I wouldn't be raving about it. What I learned from successful women is that rather than suppress or deny envy like the rest of us, they do something brilliant with it. If you learn how to react to the first twinges, you can harness its power to wonderful use. Envy is not a good place to end but it can be a great place to start.

Think of envy as a compass of sorts. An envy attack can point you directly to what you want the most.

"Envy can be enormously healthy," says Regina Barreca, professor of English and feminist theory at the University of Connecticut and author of *Sweet Revenge: The Wicked Delights of Getting Even.* "It's a pure sensation and enables you to see what your real desires are. Too often as women we're told to put our desires aside. 'I want that' is not something a girl should say."

Though I only became fully aware of the power of envy in recent years, I actually got my first hint of it when I was nine years old. I had just moved with my family to a new neighborhood and I had become friends with several girls my age who lived on the street. It was summer and we decided to put on a talent show, which mainly involved lip-synching to old records. A ten-year-old girl who lived nearby volunteered to help us, and my friends were ecstatic because this girl, Missy, was the subject of their purest adoration. During the days of rehearsal, Missy elevated me to the position of her pet, praising me and sharing her Hershey chocolate almond candy bars with me. Though this secretly thrilled me, I realized it was causing problems for a girl named Stephanie, who was Missy's biggest fan. Stephanie took to sulking, but I didn't let that stop me from wallowing in my new status. One day as I was standing on a porch lost in thought, Stephanie walked up behind me and sunk her teeth into my calf as hard as she could. I let out a yelp, then began to sob. Mothers came running and there was plenty of fuss, and Stephanie was sent to her room, probably without supper. Once I calmed down, I played the dignified martyr—quick to forgive because I knew I was partly to blame. What I also felt, I have to admit, was a certain amount of awe for Stephanie. There was something so pure and fierce about her feelings. She had wanted to be Missy's favorite, but I got in the way. When she bit me she was saying, "I hate you because you got what I wanted."

I'm not advising you to take a bite out of anyone, but envy can show you what you want—when you allow it to. If you're at one of those points in life where you're not sure what you really crave or need—you think you know what you want but the people around you are telling you it should be something different—or you've gotten what you always thought you wanted, but it's leaving you ice cold, allow yourself a fifteen-minute envy attack. Instead of ignoring or squashing the feelings like a used orange juice carton, let your envy assert itself and effortlessly point you in the direction of what you need.

Because envy is so basic and pure, it's a way to get beyond what you suspect you want—or what people are suggesting you want—and discover what you're literally aching for. Maybe it's a third child or a business of your own or a better marriage or a stint in the Peace Corps. You may not even be aware you want something until you see that someone else has it, and now you're wishing it was yours and not hers.

"The big surprise about envy," says Ann Ulanov, Ph.D., professor of psychiatry and religion at Union Theological Seminary and the author of *Cinderella and Her Sisters*, "is that it really can lead to something good. If you can stop and examine the feeling of wanting what someone else has—which takes a lot of energy—you'll find that what you're seeing in the other person's life is really a good thing. For envy, after all, is admiration gone sour. At the bottom of envy is a lavish, all-out sighting of good qualities and a registering of awe and amazement at them."

At *Redbook,* one of our most popular columns is "Ask Me Anything," written by the wise and wonderful Ellen Welty, who is a great believer in the power of envy and likens it to a little man sitting on your shoulder. "He's always telling us what we want," she says. "He says things like 'See the sexy way your friend dresses' or 'Look how easily your colleague speaks in front of groups.' The second you heed that little man, it's like a powerful shot of adrenaline. It's such a high to know what you want and then resolve to go out and get it. Suddenly you no longer feel sorry for yourself. You no longer wish evil on the person you once envied. In fact, you respect them for having what they have almost as much as you respect yourself for going for it."

A friend and colleague of mine, Mary Quinlan, told me recently that it was envy that helped her decide to adopt a child. "I had been trying for a long time to have another baby," says Quinlan, the former publisher of *New Woman*. "People think because you have one child that it shouldn't bother you as much if you can't get pregnant another time—but it does. The yearning is just as painful. And I wanted so much for my daughter to have a brother or sister.

"Eventually, my husband and I decided to try in vitro—and I conceived. We were thrilled. At about twelve weeks, though, just as I was allowing myself to relax a little bit, I lost the baby. It was such an awful experience, and at this point, I just wasn't sure what to do. Adoption was the next option to consider, but it was a big deal for me and I wasn't certain it was what I really wanted.

"Then, one day, still feeling unsure of what I wanted, I had the most remarkable revelation. It was Sunday, we were visiting Washington, D.C., and so we went to church there. During communion a woman walked up the aisle carrying her tiny baby on her shoulder. As she stood in line, her back was to me and though I couldn't see her face, I saw the baby's face as he lay against the mother's shoulder. Suddenly I was overwhelmed by envy and longing—and I started to cry. I wanted what she had so badly. That was the moment I became sure of my focus, when I knew I was ready to adopt."

Today, Quinlan has a two-year-old son she adopted from Paraguay.

The Games That Envy Plays

There's just one little hitch to all of this. "Envy can lead to something good if you can stand to experience it," says Dr. Ulanov, "but generally we can't."

Dr. Ulanov believes that most of us have a hard time admitting to what we're feeling. A friend of mine, therapist Margerie Lapp, says that one of the discoveries she's made in her counseling work is that people are extraordinarily reluctant to admit to themselves that they're envious. Lapp has to do a lot of prying to get people to the root of their anger or their disappointment. But she enjoys helping them make the discovery that envy is a major part of their anguish, because then they can right the situation and go after that which will make them happiest.

This doesn't mean that envy doesn't reveal itself—it does, but it's often wearing a disguise. Says Dr. Ulanov: "Envy rarely shows itself directly. It shows itself in a derivative way. You might denigrate someone else's achievement or damn them with faint praise. Have you ever heard the expression 'spit in the other person's soup'? It means they can have their prize but not before you try to spoil it for them."

Remember the time your good, good friend—your single girl pal who called you every day and commiserated with you whenever you had a blind date who looked like a wookie—announced on the phone that she had met a really great, cute guy who was on the partner track at a law firm? They'd gone to bed and had fabulous sex and she thought this might really be the one? As she joyfully described him, you felt a toxic spill polluting your emotional system and the urge to scream, "NO NO NO!" What did you do after you got off the phone? Did you grab a beer from the fridge, sit back in your chair, and say to yourself, "Wow, I'm really feeling envious of her. I've been dating a lot of loser artist types lately who are never going to make a dime, and now she's gone and found a sexy, personable lawyer who is making tons of dough and I wish I were her."

Not likely. You might have felt annoyed, angry, hyped-up, but you told yourself it was because your friend had been a show-off or had behaved, dare you say it, like a slut. Or maybe she'd always said she despised lawyers and you couldn't believe she was being such a hypocrite.

It's impossible to use envy to your advantage if you don't first admit you're feeling it.

12 Things You Say When You're Envious but Can't Admit It

1. "Her father knows everybody."
2. "I can't believe they gave it to her."
3. "She can talk her way into anything."
4. "I don't know what she sees in him."
5. "She'll be miserable there."
6. "She'll date anything that moves."

7. "She'll be sorry."
8. "She doesn't know what she's doing."
9. "She must be out of her mind."
10. "She's changed."
11. "I wouldn't trade places with her for the world."
12. "I couldn't care less."

Another sign that you're in the throes of envy is that the dynamics of your relationship with the other person shift. Conversations may seem awkward or you may even feel she's being cool to you—behavior you attribute to a new-found arrogance in the other person, but could actually be the result of aloofness she feels on your part.

"When someone's feeling envy, they will relate to the person differently and then the other person begins acting differently," says Lapp. "It becomes a self-fulfilling prophecy, a vicious cycle. When you hear yourself saying, 'She used to be so nice and then she changed,' it could be that *you* have changed in your behavior toward her, and she's reacting accordingly."

How to Use Envy to Help You Know What You Want

Once you admit that you are feeling envious, you can start to make good use of it. The first thing is to dig down, as Dr. Ulanov says, and find the yearning underneath. The other person's success—whether it's a baby, a man, a new life, a new job, a championship in the quilt show—has hit a nerve with you, exposed a desire of yours that hasn't been recognized or nurtured. "Now that the hunger has reared its head, you can salute it," says Dr. Ulanov.

And now that you know what's bothering you, you can take the focus off the friend or acquaintance or stranger with the goodies and put it on your own needs. You can make the envy suddenly about *you,* not her.

But there's still one other trick you need to learn: You have to know exactly what it is about the other person's victory that you *really* desire. You see, envy reveals a yearning, but sometimes that yearning is misleading. You may not envy precisely what the other person has. You may want one aspect of the prize. Or, as Dr. Ulanov suggests, you may want something that the other person's accomplishment merely symbolizes.

Ellen Welty agrees. "You think you envy another woman for her big breasts and yet what you might really want for yourself is to focus on dressing sexier."

When I was twenty-six, I was knocked over by a wave of envy the size of a tsunami. I was standing at a party chatting with a few people, when I overheard a young woman say that she was considering taking a job as the editor of a newspaper published on a luxury cruise ship during its yearlong voyage around the world. In a flash I could imagine everything about the job: She would spend her days as her own boss, collecting fun tidbits for the newspaper; her nights would be spent on the deck of the ship, wrapped in a steamer blanket and talking to men in tuxedos as the endless ocean spread out in front of them—or sitting in a tropical bar in some exotic port of call. I'd never even known such a job existed, but hearing it described, I knew I wanted it desperately and I hated her for having it.

The next day I frantically called around to all the cruise lines and asked if they had their own newspapers and needed an editor, but I turned up nothing. It's a good thing, because it really wasn't my dream job. Boats and ships not only make me mildly claustrophobic, but, if they start to rock, I tend to puke my guts out. As I got a grip on my feelings over the next few weeks, I began to realize that what I was longing for wasn't a job as the editor of a cruise ship newspaper, but simply more autonomy in my job and more adventure in my life.

So, even though you're feeling envious over someone else's achievement or victory or possession, you need to realize that you may not want the identical thing. A friend tells you over lunch about an officemate who has announced that she's leaving the company to start a business from her home that will provide soup-to-nuts assistance to people locating to the area from other countries. She plans to help them find a house in a neighborhood that's right for them, a good school for their kids, as well as hosting parties to introduce them to people in the area. You go home in a blue funk, wishing you could steal her new business right out from under her. Why? Is the idea for the business one that you've been nurturing in your mind for two years but haven't gotten around to? Or have you reacted simply to the idea of someone having the guts to start her own business? Or maybe it's something even smaller: working at home so you could have more time with the kids? Or could it even be the glamour aspect: meeting and hosting parties for lots of new people?

3 Little Questions That Help Figure Out What You're Really Passionate About

1. In one sentence, what is it you're really envying?
2. What four words sum up that thing best?
3. Of those four words, which appeals to you most?

Envy as a Kick in the Butt

Now that you've uncovered a secret yearning or gotten a wake-up call about a goal or dream you've been ignoring, you have to avoid the tendency to stew and instead put things into motion. One reason I think envy throws us into a funk is that we have this sense that if the other person has something we want, it means it's *taken,* there's none left for us. Okay, that may have been true during high school. There *was* only one homecoming queen, and if she was it, you couldn't be. But in the world at large there is generally plenty of booty to go around.

Regina Barreca tells a great story about using envy as a kick in the butt: "I owe a great deal to envy. The first piece I ever sent out for publication I wrote only because a girl I went to college with had two poems printed in a small literary journal that I happened to come across in a tiny bookstore on St. Mark's Place in Manhattan's East Village. There I was, flipping through these thin pages after cranking out another paper for graduate school, and there was her name. It tripped some internal alarm signal, her name in print, and all my sirens were immediately set off. I had to do better. For God's sake, I had to do at least as well.

"To make a long story short, I got one poem published, one I wrote with my eyes more on her words than on my own. Envy took me down the dark road of my own ambition and gave me the necessary gall to toss a typed page on an editor's desk."

Be Flexible with Your Envy

Sometimes envy points you nicely toward what you're craving, and you start out after it, but things unfold differently from what you expected. You've got to be willing to improvise.

Several years ago I went to dinner at the home of a friend who had just spent three months combining her two-bedroom apartment with the one-bedroom apartment next door that she and her husband had just purchased. I had listened to her war stories during construction, looked at fabric swatches, applauded her victories with contractors, and now I was dying to see the results. It wasn't simply a matter of curiosity. This is a friend whose pleasure gives me pleasure, and I looked forward to how happy I'd feel when I saw the success of her labors.

Boy, was I shocked by my reaction when I finished the tour of her newly improved apartment. Yes, I was thrilled for her, but I also felt downright envious. The place was freaking great. She suddenly had a gorgeous formal dining room, and a family room that everyone could sprawl around in. Her place had gone from adequate in size to rambling. We had a nice evening, but as I walked home along the Manhattan streets, I could barely refrain from whimpering.

Because my envy was so pathetically obvious, it was easy to get past it and focus on myself, on why I was having such a reaction. Over the next few days, I realized that for several years I'd been ignoring the fact that my husband, kids, and I had totally outgrown our apartment and that living in it was really making me miserable. Typical of apartments in New York high-rise buildings, it had a very tiny kitchen with almost no counter space, which made cooking family meals a hassle and turned entertaining into a nightmare. Because we had no family room, the kids were forever being told to keep their toys in their bedroom or stop bouncing around the living room, where, by the way, the dog had managed to strip apart the couch, so that it looked like the DEA had been in the apartment doing a search for heroin. Our bedroom functioned as a home office, and the first thing I gazed at when I opened my eyes in the morning was a fax machine and reams of paper everywhere. Seeing my friend's home made me realize that I craved something bigger, calmer, and more accommodating.

Actually, I didn't want just any big apartment. I could suddenly see that the perfect solution for us would be to

combine our apartment with the one-bedroom next door—
just as my friend had done.

There were all sorts of reasons why this was a brilliant
idea. We liked our building, and now we could stay in it.
We'd save lots of money on moving costs. The resale value
of the combined apartments would be significantly greater
than if each apartment were sold separately. And there was
one other funny advantage. Whereas some people have
recurring dreams about being naked in public or not
preparing for an exam, mine was that I would suddenly discover one day that my home has several extra rooms that
I wasn't aware of. Who knew what psychic benefit would
come from living out a dream fantasy.

Now the only thing I had to do was convince the older
couple next door that they should sell to us. Their apartment had nose-dived in value in recent years, and I sus-
pected they would jump at the chance to sell it for a fair
price. I started engaging in lots of visualization exercises,
including staring positively at the wall between our two
homes. When I first broached the subject, the woman
sounded mildly interested and told me to check back with
her in a few months when she would give me a more defin-
itive answer.

And for the next two years that's how it went. I'd inquire
and she'd exhibit interest, but then put me off. "Maybe this
summer." "Check with me in the fall." Have you ever seen
a dog follow a little kid who's holding a doughnut or
cookie, and the dog's tongue is hanging out and he can't
take his eyes off the doughnut and he moves along with the
kid just hoping the doughnut will fall on the ground so he

can snatch it? That's how I felt. The prize seemed torturously just out of my reach. But I knew what I wanted and I didn't want to fold my campaign.

Finally, I had an epiphany. I realized that I was being held hostage by the original object of my envy—the magic that can happen when two adjoining apartments are combined—and that I had to break away. What was needed on my part was some flexibility. My husband and I talked it over and decided that we had nothing to lose by seeing what was available on the outside. He made an appointment with a real estate broker. Two days later we met with her to tour two apartments and a town house. We had absolutely no interest in a town house, but the agent thought it would at least help her get an idea of our taste.

Much to our shock, we fell in love with the town house, and put a bid on it that weekend. It took me a week to adjust to the idea that I wasn't going to be buying the apartment next door. The irony is that one week after we made the bid, our neighbor decided that she really did want to sell. After I told her the news she never spoke to me again.

It was relatively easy for me to be flexible with my envy, to shift gears and embrace the idea of a different kind of home, because basically all I really wanted was a place in which I could turn around and not see a product made by Little Tikes.

Sometimes it's harder to be flexible because the specific thing you want doesn't come in other varieties, or it does but they're unappealing at first glance. A friend of mine confessed to me lately that she realized that for years she had desperately envied the kind of close friendship I had with my mother. She wanted such a relationship, but her mother is cold, self-absorbed, extremely needy, and yet at the same time dismissive of the affection my friend offers. My friend tried everything to make it happen.

She went to a therapist and followed the recommended approaches. She thought a lot about her mother and considered ways they might connect. She rejoiced when she was pregnant because she thought being a grandmother would allow her mother to show affection for her once removed. But her mother remained cold and totally disinterested in her grandchild.

After a long, long time my friend accepted it was not going to happen the way she had hoped. She also recognized how much love her mother-in-law had been showering on her in recent years. It wasn't a mother's love, it wasn't what she longed for, but since she finally realized that she would never get the other, she embraced it.

And If You Don't Feel Any Envy, Try Conjuring Some Up

Nothing lately has turned you green? Look around, see what you would steal if you could. I sometimes feel I married the right guy the second time because I scanned the horizon to see which of my friends had marriages that really appealed to me. After I got divorced at thirty-one, I heard an expert say that most individuals marry the same person all over again. I certainly didn't want to do that—it would have been like that eerie "Twilight Zone" episode in which a group of people take off these hideous rubber masks and discover that their faces are now shaped exactly like the masks.

So I spent some time thinking about my friends' marriages and whose I admired most. The relationship I found myself envying surprised me. The guy wasn't exactly a dreamboat and he sometimes helped out around the house with a dish towel tucked in the front of his pants like an old geezer working at a coffee shop. But he adored my friend, loved to spend Saturday afternoons with her in the park, and lovingly listened to her stories. I thought, "This is what I'm going after—even if it comes with a dish towel tucked in the pants."

Glance around, focus, let yourself project. You may discover that if you allow for a little envy, you'll end up with a clearer idea of your passion.

And if you don't, proceed to the next chapter.

2

BITE OFF MORE THAN
YOU CAN CHEW

Okay, maybe you're not the envious kind of girl. You read the previous chapter, and you were perfectly willing to discover what your passion was by lusting after someone else's life or accomplishment, but you just couldn't feel the least bit covetous. Or maybe you *are* the envious type, but right now nothing is making you feel ready to kill. There is, fortunately, another technique available for discovering what you want this year, this moment, but I offer it with a warning: Unlike envy, it is not something you can do from the comfort of a club chair in your home while enjoying some dry white wine and a bag of sour cream and onion–flavored potato chips. This one will take some work.

If you are still unsure of what you want, you must get off your duff and get out into the world and search until you bump into it. You must prowl, explore, snoop, poke, and peek, investing lots of time and energy. In other words, you must take classes, read dozens of books and magazine articles, search the outer reaches of cyberspace, eat lunch with a wide variety of people—some of whom may know something that will make a difference to you. Make calls to friends of friends of friends, and follow up on the teeniest of leads. And you must do all of this knowing that many of your efforts will produce nothing more than pinched toes and frustration. This is a strategy that I see used over and over again by women who get what they want. Diane Sawyer calls it being "a mercenary for experience." Because somewhere in the process of all this tireless, ruthless collecting of information, you *will* find what you want.

Why This Isn't as Ass Backward as It Sounds

I know this seems like a totally backward way to go about finding what you want, because if the yearning is inside of you, wouldn't it be better to plumb the depths in search of it? Books on finding one's calling in life always seem to suggest that you cogitate and soul-search in the privacy of your own home. But yearnings can be unformed, vague, slippery. Often you don't know what you want until one day you walk into the right room and see it there in front of you. Even if you have a good sense of your talents and skills, you may not be aware of the right application for you. For so many of the successful women I've met, discovering what they want in life isn't a matter of waking up one morning and shouting "Eureka" but rather going through a process of elimination.

That was the case for Susan Molinari, the former congresswoman from Staten Island, New York, who delivered the keynote address at the Republican National Convention in 1996 and who recently left office before her term was up to become coanchor for *Saturday Morning* on CBS.

"I don't think I've ever had a defining moment when I've woken up and said, 'This is what I want to do,'" says Molinari. "Instead, I think I work toward opportunities, and then when they present themselves, I decide to take them or not to take them, based on whether I can live with myself if I didn't try."

Not very romantic, is it? How much nicer to have this great passion from the time you were six to win a gold medal in the freestyle and then work toward it every day. Yet the women I've met who have what they want aren't hopeless romantics about their destiny. They accept the fact that you aren't necessarily born knowing what you want, that you may have to go out there and find it.

They also know that there are probably lots of things that they could do, and that it's just fine to throw themselves into one (at least for a while) without agonizing about whether something else would be better.

You know the fun and whimsical clothes by fashion designer Cynthia Rowley, the ones worn by celebs like Natalie Merchant, Claire Danes, and Sarah Jessica Parker?

It's no wonder her clothes look the way they do; Rowley herself is dynamic, captivating, zany, and obviously in love with what she does. She created her first dress at age seven, making the pattern by lying on a piece of paper and tracing herself on it, but she never planned, while growing up, to be a fashion designer, much less one who would win the Council of Fashion Designers' Perry Ellis Award for new fashion talent. She sort of stumbled on it as a career.

"I always thought that I would be an artist and I studied fine arts at the Art Institute of Chicago," she says. "I didn't even know until much later, until I was in school, that fashion was even an option. I come from a family of artists and so I always drew and painted. I sewed because I just thought that's how you make clothes. I grew up in a really small town in the Midwest, and there weren't any stores to shop in—there was a Sears, but it was an hour away.

"I just wanted to make things, to create things. Even when I went into fashion as an adult, it was just a means of being creative. It was just a different medium from painting or drawing. I would be happy making furniture or designing bicycles."

So don't get hung up on the idea that there's only one perfect thing to do or love, one perfect place to live. And you also can't sit there waiting for inspiration to arrive at your door as Robert Kincaid did in Robert James Waller's *Bridges of Madison County.* In the end all poor Francesca got was two days of fantastic sex in one lifetime. Now is the moment to go searching for what you truly want, for what will complete you.

6 Sort of Obvious Things to Try (But Hey, They Can't Hurt)

You are now poised to become a mercenary for experience. You do not need a machete or a submachine gun or face paint to make you look like jungle undergrowth. You simply need to get out the door.

But where do you *go?* As mundane as it sounds, you're best off starting with the obvious. Though you may feel clueless about precisely what it is you want, you nonetheless should have at least a vague notion of what your aspirations are. At the very least, you should know where in your life you're feeling needy—home, men, work, friends. That's the starting point for your mercenary work. If, for instance, you have a sense you would like to start a business from your home and never again report to anyone even resembling your current boss, the obvious mercenary work you need to do is find the statewide organization of women entrepreneurs, go to a meeting, talk to as many members as possible, and get a sense of what is involved and what some of the businesses are that might inspire you.

Some basic strategies that can often prove enlightening:

1. Take a class in something you suspect has the power to move you.
2. Talk to three people who have succeeded in the area in which you're interested.
3. Get on the Internet and explore the topic.
4. Try to get an exploratory interview with someone who knows something.

5. Buy a composition book, go to a Starbucks, order a cappuccino, and write in a stream of consciousness style, starting with what you vaguely think you want and letting words take you to the prize—your heart's real desire.
6. Talk into a tape recorder about what you think you want and then listen to what you've said.

11 Slightly Wacky Things to Do, Too

Taking the obvious paths is important. But that's not always enough. I also believe that one of the best strategies to discovering what's missing in your life is to try the unusual, the offbeat, the silly, and the adventurous. This can bring any secret yearnings into the light of day.

1. Go to lunch with a good but casual friend (*not* one of your very best friends and *not* someone you work with) and ask her, "If you could picture me doing something with my life that would make me really happy, what would it be?"
2. Take a long walk by yourself in a quiet area and think about three times in your life when you were truly exhilarated. When you get home, jot them down.
3. Go to the library and get out a big stack of *Condé Nast Traveler* magazines and look at the last page of each issue, which is a regular feature called "Room with a View" (the page is a photo of a breathtaking view from the window of a certain room in a hotel). Go through all of

them and pick your three favorites. Pin them up on a bulletin board or your refrigerator. What might they be able to tell you?

4. Plan a dinner party and invite a few people you know, as well as several people you've met but haven't had a chance to get to know. Ask them questions about their lives, what do they enjoy, what do they want to do next?

5. Over a period of several weeks, avoid talking about yourself and ask people lots of questions about themselves.

6. Buy one of those little notebooks with blank pages and a pretty cover and, before you go to bed, write down the one thing you enjoyed the most about the day.

7. Make a list of your three happiest vacations. What do they have in common?

8. What are the three things you're best at? Create a profile of someone who has those three skills or talents. What does she do for a living? What are her leisure activities? What sorts of people does she enjoy being with?

9. Jot down the four or five things people most compliment you on (such as "You're so organized" or "You're so good with people").

10. List three times in the last year when you did something that made you feel gloriously satisfied.

11. Plan an afternoon in which you do something you've never tried before just because it sounds intriguing, even though it's not quite you—like going to the rodeo or having a reflexology session. Afterward, write down what you liked about it that you didn't expect.

Stepping Back

Now you've got all this information from your various excursions—what is it trying to tell you? You have to step back and see the pattern in the things you enjoy.

I learned a fascinating lesson last year when I hired someone to help me make some decorating changes in a farmhouse my husband and I own in Pennsylvania. When we first got the house eight years ago, I was forced to go on a manic shopping spree for furniture and trimmings because we didn't have a stick of extra stuff. I relied heavily on the color green, choosing fabrics in both florals and little prints. Why green? I happened to find some fabrics in green that were pretty. Though I have decent taste—I can look at shag carpeting and recognize that it goes against the laws of nature—I just don't have any flair for putting a room together. Eventually I hired a decorator, someone whose specialty was helping clients work with existing possessions. She made a bunch of suggestions, one of which was that I should paint all the walls various shades of off-white, with names like "coffee" and "cameo," and that I should remove some of the prints and paintings from the walls ("too busy"). I followed her advice and the rooms did look more pulled together. But over time I began to see that they were unbelievably dull. I realized one day that my house bore a distinct resemblance to a giant pair of tan chinos.

The longer I lived in the space, the more it bothered me. I knew I needed to do something, but I wasn't sure what.

I ordered cute knickknacks from catalogs and tried to add touches of color, but nothing worked. Eventually I heard of a woman in the area named Denny Daikeler who was widely known as a kind of decorating doctor, and I begged her to come by and give me her advice.

Before she even made a single suggestion, Denny told me to go through lots of decorating magazines and pull out pictures of rooms I loved. She told me to tape all the pictures into a large artist's sketchbook and, where possible, note what I liked in the margins. Then she would analyze what I had found.

After I was finished, she took the book home with her and studied my choices. Her conclusions were so obvious from the pictures I'd chosen, but I hadn't recognized them—even at the time I was ripping and pasting. Though I had picked green as a base color for my home, my true passion appeared to be for much bolder and brighter colors—reds and oranges and yellows and purples. I loved color on walls. In fact, practically every page of my fantasy book featured colorful walls with white trim—and yet my own house was filled with beige walls. I seemed to love checks and stripes, not florals. And I obviously preferred lots of objects around me—paintings, books, vases of flowers, primitive statues, bowls of fruit, and the like. My own house was spare, with little on the walls and shelves.

At the decorating doctor's suggestion, I began to change my rooms, and I adored the results. The kitchen, which had white-washed cabinets, off-white walls, and a maroon-painted wood floor, got painted red. Yellow curtains were added and—get this—a country-tile floor in purple. I walk down to this whimsical kitchen in the morning and it makes me so happy.

Now, I'd certainly *seen* all of these colors together before, but it was only when I'd finished my sketchbook project that I realized how much I liked them in a room. That exercise made me see how important it is to step back and really *see* the connection among the things that satisfy and energize you. And then you need to analyze what that tells you.

- When you listen to people talk about their experiences, what seems most alluring?
- When you gaze at all those views, what do the three you like best have in common?
- As you glance over what you've written about your favorite moments and vacations and experiences, what do they have in common?
- Where's the intersection of what you see as your particular skills and those other people see? What really makes your heart sing?

4 Signs You're onto Something

1. You can't stop thinking about it.
2. You can't fall asleep when you're thinking about it.
3. You want to talk to people about it but don't because you're afraid someone will steal it.
4. You feel an urge to date it.

Still Feeling Absolutely No Sense of What You Want? Proceed to the Next 7 Steps

You've been out and about for weeks now, reading, looking, listening, studying, gathering, investigating, jotting down, reviewing, considering the connections. Maybe a lightbulb went on, but you still haven't been able to see it because you're so used to wearing dark glasses.

1. Look Behind You

When you're going through the process of trying to discover what you want, it may help to look to your past. Was there once something that made you very happy but got left along the side of the road because you thought you were finished with it or had outgrown it? Perhaps you laid it aside because you felt sure you would find more important and exciting things along the way to your ever-evolving future. A friend of mine, a dazzling and beautiful twenty-eight-year-old woman named Jane Rinzler, started a business she's passionate about by finally recognizing that she had actually stumbled on her calling at sixteen. Today she's president of her own research company, Youth Intelligence, a marketing consulting company specializing in tracking trends among teens and twentysomethings. Her clients have included Revlon, Heineken, and Nike.

After graduating from college, Rinzler started a career in advertising on what's known as the "account side," dealing with clients and overseeing the development of ad campaigns. She quickly discovered that she hated it.

"I just didn't look forward to going in every day," she says. "I was working on Pizza Hut, and it was horrible—lots of people obsessing about how many pepperoni do you show on the pizza in the commercial. Of course, there are lots of people who love this kind of work, and I thought, 'Well, maybe it's the agency that's wrong for me or maybe it's the account, let me try another.' I never thought, 'Maybe I don't like the work or maybe I'm not as good at it as I should be.'"

She started searching for a job. As she explored other opportunities, she began to have a niggling sense that the account side of the business wasn't for her. At one agency where she interviewed, the players admitted that they weren't exactly sure what they were looking for—maybe it was an account person or perhaps what they really needed was a research person. There was some tentative interest in starting a new division to interpret consumer needs in a fresh way. Jane felt her heart skip a beat with excitement. She knew this was something she wanted to do—in fact, it was actually something she'd loved doing years before.

You see, since high school, Jane had been fascinated with her generation's desires and motives. When she was sixteen, her mother, a book reviewer, asked Jane's opinion of a book by a forty-year-old psychologist. The book sought to explain what was going on in the heads of teenagers and got it all wrong.

"I read it," Jane remembers, "and thought, 'He just doesn't get it.'" Then she thought, "Oh my God, everyone in the world is going to read this and they are not going to understand kids my age. His approach is absolutely wrong. He's asking questions like 'What do you think of marriage?' instead of asking 'How many times are you going to get married?' It wasn't that he was purposely being wrong, but rather he was looking through a lens that reflected what his life had been at fifteen. But so many things had changed. Baby boomers had unwanted pregnancies to deal with, we had AIDS. Baby boomers saw people land on the moon, we saw the *Challenger* blow up."

When Jane's mother asked her "Could you do it better?" she said yes, and set out to write her own book. It was called *Teens Speak Out, a Report from Today's Teens on Their Most Intimate Thoughts, Feelings, and Hopes for the Future* and was published in 1986.

Jane took the job with the new agency, and set up a research department to explain to advertisers what teens were thinking and how to reach them. Eventually she decided to go out on her own—and she has been wildly happy ever since. She found her passion by looking behind her. "I am not passionate about a lot of things," says Jane, "but I have a real passion for explaining my generation because I truly feel people misunderstand us. But it took me a long time to realize that not everyone could do that."

2. Get Out of Town

Sometimes what's holding you back from seeing what you want are the plans and expectations everybody else has for you. Indeed, you may be relying on them to keep you from having to come up with your own plans and expectations. There is only one solution for that: Get the hell out of town. You must leave the scene so that you can stop hearing old ideas and be inspired by something brand new.

Several months ago I had lunch with one of the most successful plus-size models in the country, Emme Aronson. She is really gorgeous—in fact, *People* magazine named her one of the fifty most beautiful people in America in 1996. She told me she owes her success to leaving the East Coast where she'd grown up and heading out to California with her college roommate, where she was finally away from her stepfather's destructive messages.

The constant theme he offered while she was growing up was that her weight was a problem. When she was twelve he made her strip to her underwear one day and then he used a black Magic Marker to draw circles on the parts of her arms and legs he considered "trouble spots"—where she was going to get fat if she wasn't careful. She tried to scrub the spots off, but later, when she was at the neighborhood pool, kids began to laugh and she realized that the marks were still visible. It was an utterly humiliating experience.

While she was in college, at Syracuse University, her roommate and she arranged to spend the summer after graduation working as baby-sitters in L.A. for the roommate's uncle, who was in the entertainment business. The kids were a handful and the arrangement didn't last long, but when she was in L.A., people told her they liked the way she looked. It was a whole new way of seeing herself. She landed a job as a page at NBC, later moved to a position as on-air talent at a television station, and eventually worked her way back to New York and the world of plus-size modeling.

3. Give Serendipity a Chance

Stop concentrating so hard on what you need and just let life take over for a few weeks. But you've got to be *out there* for serendipity to happen. Catherine Cook, a landscape designer in Connecticut, has a remarkable story on how serendipity led her to love. It was ten years ago. She was running her own, ever-expanding photo retouching studio in New York City, working long, long days and feeling exhausted and empty. She was desperate for a rest, for some kind of sabbatical.

When friends suggested she join them on a hike in New Zealand, she decided that was the reprieve she'd been looking for. She'd broken off a romantic relationship the summer before and she had nothing on that front holding her back.

"My friends and I were going to hike together for a week," says Catherine, "but then I was going to travel around on my own—for a couple of months. I knew I was walking into the unknown, but I felt that doing so would help me get back to a creative frame of mind. I'm a believer that leaving some things to serendipity allows you to open up other, exciting avenues."

She hiked with her friends and then she was on her own. One day, while traveling by rented car on a curvy, lonely mountain road, she spotted a hitchhiker and decided to pick him up. She didn't ever do that sort of thing, but there was so little traffic, she knew it might be an hour before another car passed. And she had already discovered that New Zealand is a country in which people open themselves up to others that way.

He turned out to be an English dairy farmer studying dairies in New Zealand for a few months. They were inseparable that day, and soon they knew they were in love. They've been married ten years and work together today in their own business.

4. Ask for Advice (But Be Very Very Careful)

One of the things I've noticed about women who get what they want is that they often have a personal advisory board on which they can rely for guidance. I don't mean a mentor, by the way. Having a mentor is wonderful, but there's no guarantee you can find one even if you want one, and if you do, you really shouldn't put all your eggs in one basket. The guy who hired you and nurtured you along in business is not the person you should turn to for advice when you're wondering if you should go back to school and study to be a midwife. He will think that idea stinks. Plus, your mentor may move on and then where does that leave you? Better to have a mix of people, who can offer a wide range of perspectives. Include a former boss or two, the woman who took you under her wing the summer you lived in London, your mother, and so on.

Your personal advisory board members are there to guide you in a crisis and offer input when you must make a tough decision, but they can also help when you're stuck wondering what you want. They may see certain wonderful traits you're ignoring or understand better than you do what's missing in your life.

Through my job at *Redbook* I got to talk to a fabulous young trial lawyer named Suzelle Smith who has her own firm in Los Angeles. We profiled her in an article called "Winning on Appeal: The Hot New Breed of Female Lawyers." After law school, Smith joined a tiny corporate law firm. "I thought I wanted to be a corporate lawyer," she says, "because I liked the idea of sitting around telling businessmen what to do. But one day a mentor of mine told me, 'You may not know this, but you have the right skills to be a trial lawyer. You like to debate, to challenge, you're good on your feet, you like to interact with people.'"

It was a defining moment in her life. "Sometimes," she says, "people who really know you can see better than you can what you should do."

When handbag designer Kate Spade was trying to decide what kind of business she should start, she considered almost everything, including opening a Mexican restaurant. It was her future husband who suggested handbags. "I'm a handbag freak," she says. "I had a thousand handbags in my closet, but it never occurred to me that I could make a business out of my passion until he said it."

Why can others see what you can't? Because they've got needed perspective along with a cool head and a fresh eye.

If no one volunteers this information, don't be afraid to ask. But *don't* whine. Say, "I'm feeling a little frustrated these days and I don't know why. Is there something you think I'm not seeing or taking hold of right now? What do you think I should be doing that I'm not?"

But you must choose your advisers well. There is nothing more dangerous than asking the wrong person for input.

Probably the worst story I've ever heard about this particular hazard was one I was told by Nancy Taylor Rosenberg, the mega-best-selling author of legal thrillers, including *Mitigating Circumstances* and *Interest of Justice*.

When her kids were young, she and her husband were having some pretty serious money problems. Rosenberg decided to try writing a crime thriller. When she finished the novel, she asked a neighbor if she'd read it and give her opinion. Weeks went by and the woman said nothing. Finally, after several months, Rosenberg asked the neighbor if she had the manuscript. The woman said, "Yeah," and handed it back to her without a word. Rosenberg stuck the book in a drawer and made no attempt to get it published.

In 1992, many years later, while recovering from an injury, she wrote *Mitigating Circumstances*. It sold at auction for $787,000.

"It drives me crazy," says Rosenberg, "to think that my first novel could have been successful if only I hadn't been so terrified to show it to someone who knew more than my next-door neighbor. I believe I had the same writing qualities then as I do now. I could have realized my dream and avoided all those years of struggle and despair."

You should never ask advice from:

• People who don't really know you.
• People who know you but aren't truly supportive.

- Colleagues at work (even if you sense your restlessness is not specifically about work).
- Relatives who have a preconceived notion of who you are and what you need.
- Friends who have a stake in keeping you right where you are.
- Anyone with an ax to grind.
- Anyone who will condone your attempts to stall, postpone, not try.

There are three good indicators of someone who deserves to be on your advisory board:

1. They happily conduct a big Q&A session with you, asking questions that draw you out and help you see your real motives and concerns.
2. They do not constantly reference back everything you say to *their* experience.
3. They give you their opinion only after careful consideration.

5. Pull Out a Hip-Pocket Dream

When I talked to Nancy Taylor Rosenberg, she mentioned that being a novelist had been "a hip-pocket dream" for her—something that she'd always longed for but had stuck in a back pocket because she had three kids to raise and couldn't afford to give up her job. Many of us have hip-pocket dreams. Now is a good time to bring them out into the light of day. Are you ready to go after them? Could you try some permutations?

When Tobey Gifford, the national aerobics champion, was in high school, she dreamed of doing something great with her life. She loved gymnastics, and saw that as part of her future—as well as college—but at nineteen she found herself pregnant.

"I was so scared," she says. "What was I going to do? My life was turned upside down."

She married the father and put her dreams on hold. She went to school part-time for nursing, and eventually coached kids in gymnastics in after-school programs. Because she felt out of shape, she began taking body-sculpting classes and aerobics training. She soon began to teach and after two years stepped into competition. For her it was a chance to pull out the hip-pocket dream. "I always felt I hadn't hung on to the gymnastics long enough. This has given me the chance to see something all the way through."

6. Take a Leap

Sometimes, when you have an inkling of what you want, there's no way to know for sure beforehand that it's right for you. You have to leap first and ask questions later. Wanda Urbanska, author of *Simple Living,* was a successful writer and editor living in Los Angeles when she and her husband decided to move to Mount Airy, North Carolina, to run his parents' cherry orchard. It turned out to be a wonderful decision. She works out of a charming office overlooking Main Street and has become a spokesperson for getting off the fast track—she will be the host of an upcoming PBS series on the subject. But when the opportunity to leave L.A. because of a death in her husband's family first arose, it was awfully tough to make the decision. She had plenty of success in Los Angeles, as did her husband, a screenwriter. All she had to go on was an inkling that living in a small town could be a life change worth making even though they would be leaving behind so much. "It was an improbable choice," Urbanska says. "My journalist friends said it was a horrible idea and my mind would turn to mush. Finally I realized that I wouldn't know until I tried it."

It was only in taking the leap that she could see for sure what she really wanted.

7. Return to "6 Sort of Obvious Things to Try" (page 39)

If you're still baffled about what you want, you must continue your work as a mercenary for experience. You must read more books, take more classes, talk to more people, gaze out more windows, and ask yourself more questions. The answer will come to you sooner or later.

How to Deal with That Dead-End Feeling

When you get out of the house and start bustling about in search of what you want in life, there will be times when you return at the end of the day feeling miserable. Perhaps, in your quest, you only spoke to brusque, nasty people or perhaps you wasted a humongous amount of time racing to the end of a road that led nowhere.

There are a couple of ways to keep from feeling discouraged. One is to accept the fact that dead-end experiences sometimes have a nice way of returning dividends.

Perhaps, as a mercenary for experience, you take several courses in graphic design only to discover that you have no real talent in that area. It seems like a waste of time and money. But fast-forward to seven years later when the courses come in quite handy as you are designing posters for your campaign for the state assembly or as the cochair of your school's fall festival.

During my twenties, while I was working as a junior writer in magazines, I began to wonder if my secret desire wasn't to be a television producer or, better yet, the next Barbara Walters. I knew a career change would involve starting at the bottom again. After slowly moving up a few notches in the magazine business, I wanted to be absolutely sure I was pursuing the right path before I took the plunge. I attended several TV seminars and then I volunteered at a city-run cable TV station in New York. Soon after I started, I was tapped to be a floor manager for one of the evening shows—that's the person who signals to the on-camera people that they have five minutes left. Eventually, I was asked to anchor a once-a-week community news program.

I was delirious with excitement—*at first*—but as the night got closer, I became petrified. I had this awful sense that my terror would somehow reveal itself on the air—and boy, did it! As soon as I stared into the camera and started reading the news items my mouth became utterly dry. I swallowed every four seconds to try to relieve my discomfort. When I reviewed the tape later, I resembled a python swallowing a gazelle.

Over time, I did improve, but it was quite obvious I wasn't going to be the next Barbara Walters. It also turned out that though I liked television, I didn't really like it as much as magazines. After several years of volunteering at two stations, I decided to call it quits.

Still, it wasn't a total waste of time. As a magazine editor, I'm on television a lot and my experiences in front of and behind the camera have helped me feel more relaxed.

To keep from feeling discouraged by dead ends and major time commitments that don't produce anything concrete, I use a principle I call the Blind Date Rule of Six. In order to end up on a blind date with a really cute guy with a good job who arrives wearing decent clothes and wants to hear all about you, you must have blind dates with at least six idiots who wear jackets that say Members Only and talk about themselves without ever actually making eye contact. At the end of the evening these fellas will still feel entitled to stick a tongue down your throat.

I learned this in my early thirties, after I'd gotten divorced. I swore I wouldn't resort to blind dates, but it soon became clear that I didn't have much choice. Unless I wanted to hit the bars, this was the most expedient way to meet a guy. So I told everyone I knew that I was willing to be fixed up. Over the next three years I had dozens of blind dates, many of them experiences of pure torture. There were jerks, serious jerks, and, even worse, crashing bores. One night I actually fell asleep with my eyes partially open during dinner with a particularly tiresome guy. My contact lenses dried to my eyes. He took me home at 10:30, but I had to spend the next two hours flushing out my eyeballs so my contacts would come unstuck.

Initially it all seemed so pathetic and hopeless, but over time an interesting pattern emerged. After a run of jerks, someone really wonderful would walk over to the table in the restaurant where I was waiting, stick out his hand, and say, "You must be Kate." My calculations aren't scientific, but I'd say there was one good blind date for every six lousy ones. It makes perfect sense. There are a lot of jerks in the world, but there's a percentage of good guys, too. Sooner or later the good ones will turn up, you just have to be patient and accept the six bad dates as part of the process.

And that's what you must do when you reach dead ends and spend wasted hours during your search. Accept that failure is part of the process. When you feel discouraged, tell yourself that you must get through at least six dead ends before something good can happen.

When in Doubt, Simply Get Out of the House

I had a lightbulb go off last year in a wonderful way. For several months I'd had this low-grade restlessness and sense of longing, as if there was something missing in my life, but I couldn't put my finger on it. Because we were moving from our apartment to a new house, I assumed it might be related to the stress of relocating (you've been there, so you know what I'm talking about), and because of the move, I didn't have any time to investigate it further.

The first week in the new house was absolutely nutty. Not only was I dealing with change and confusion, with boxes everywhere, but I'd also discovered the one big flaw in the house: It had minuscule closet space and as I unpacked my clothes, I had to stack them like firewood around the perimeter of my bedroom.

In the middle of all this chaos, our eighty-five-year-old next-door neighbor stopped by to introduce herself and ask me if I'd like to accompany her the next week to a meeting of the National Society of Women Geographers. I had to fight third-degree stress and the urge to scream, "*What*—are you out of your mind?" But I smiled sweetly and very politely explained why I couldn't. Yet, even as I was saying "I won't be able to," I felt a sea change. So instead I backtracked and said, "Well, maybe if I shift a few things around I can." It had been ages since I'd done anything out of the ordinary, anything that made me a mercenary for experience, and I guess deep down part of me wanted to go.

The day arrived and I frantically left the office, wondering, as I headed uptown to the Explorers' Club, what had possessed me to do this when I should have been buying a toilet-paper dispenser. The luncheon included a slide presentation by a woman author on a remarkable Turkish writer. There were slides of the writer's hometown and the inside of her home and numerous shots of Turkey from many years ago. As I was watching, I experienced the most delicious and unexpected pleasure.

Later, as I left the Explorers' Club, I knew that what I'd been longing for was a little adventure in my life. Before I'd gotten married and had kids, I'd traveled every year to exotic places. When I wasn't traveling, I'd go on little adventures in New York City—I'd wander around Greenwich Village or the East Village or Chinatown, eat in some out-of-the-way restaurant, just relish the sights, the sounds, the *smells*. I realized that what I wanted was a little taste of adventure. I couldn't fly off to Istanbul any time soon, but I could experience those important mini-adventures again.

When you haven't a clue where you should go to find out what you want, just open the door and head down the street.

3

DON'T WAIT FOR THE RIGHT MOMENT

I hope you're feeling itchy right now. When you started reading you may not have known what you were secretly craving, but by allowing yourself to have an envy attack or by becoming a mercenary for experience, hopefully you have some idea of what is missing in your life. If so, you're ready for action.

On the other hand, maybe you already know what you want and you skipped over the last two chapters, eager for the nitty-gritty. Well, here it is. Here's where you take the first steps to getting what you want.

Actually, you probably already know what I'm going to tell you to do. You've read enough articles and seen enough interviews with self-help experts to know that this is the moment when you're encouraged to draw up the perfect game plan on how to accomplish your mission. (The books

61

I've read on getting what you want in life have all suggested that now is when you need to break open a fresh pack of 3×5 cards and plot your strategy or fill out a complicated chart in the back of the book.) And as you draw up your plan, you're supposed to determine each and every step you must take (and when).

Well, guess what? *I'm* not going to tell you to work on a big master plan, because when I look at women who are brilliant at getting what they want, they never seem to get caught up in mapping out intricate strategies. I don't mean that they head out without any sense of where they're going. But rather than getting caught up in lots of planning and pussyfooting around, they *pounce*. While the rest of us are curled up on the couch with a yellow legal pad and a fresh Rolling Writer, considering contingencies, they're already out the door and after what they want. These women start in the middle rather than the beginning, they keep their eyes open for unexpected opportunities instead of placing all their ducks in a row, and they *never* wait for the right moment.

Does that sound reckless, even downright stupid? At first glance, perhaps. But, trust me. If you're going to get what you want, you're going to have to spend less time thinking about the perfect approach and more time just doing it. And you may have to jump before you're ready. There's an old adage that goes "All glory comes from daring to begin."

The Danger of the Perfect Plan

What's so bad about developing the perfect plan? Nothing, as long as it remains flexible—a true work-in-progress that can be modified, even totally ignored at times. And you *do* need to have an idea where you're headed; you don't want to go off totally half-cocked. It's even good to write down your mission on a piece of paper. The other day, as I was going through an old notebook, I was amused to find a slip of paper that had held my New Year's resolutions from a year in the early eighties. Though I hadn't accomplished everything on my list, I had pulled off the most important ones that year: go to Rio and learn to wear contact lenses. Writing things down can help make them become a reality.

But there are problems, I've found, with getting too caught up in the planning phase.

For starters, the perfect plan keeps you busy thinking rather than doing.

Former congresswoman Susan Molinari says that she's come to believe that many women have a tendency to think about things too much. "We wonder what's the best way and how do I get myself ready," she says, "while men just say, 'I'm going to do it.' Women need to stop thinking about it and just go out there."

Betsy Myers, former deputy assistant to President Clinton, says that she thinks women get caught up in "what if?" because they're afraid of making mistakes and looking foolish.

63

"You need to do your groundwork," she says. "But then you need to dive in."

The perfect plan also has too many steps. In order to have a plan that looks and sounds thorough, it's tempting to throw in every suggestion you've ever heard. But more than half of them may be a waste of time.

Then, too, the perfect plan discourages you from pouncing on wonderful opportunities coming from left field.

Finally, the perfect plan can be an excuse for not leaping. Going after what you want is exhilarating, but it's also scary and confusing. Developing an elaborate plan can be a nice way to postpone the scary, confusing stuff.

If you want to reach your goal in this lifetime, you have to be like the women who get what they want: Start pouncing.

The Day I Learned to Pounce

For years I was a plotter and a planner. I can still vividly recall the day I saw the error of my ways.

It was the mid-eighties and I had become the executive editor in charge of articles for *Mademoiselle* magazine, with a staff of eight reporting to me. Eventually I hired this talented, nervy woman as a senior editor in my department. Jamie was young for the job—about twenty-six, I think—but fabulous at getting the top writers to work for us. How, at twenty-six, did she even *know* top writers? Because when she was only an editorial assistant at a major men's magazine, she made a point of befriending them when they came to see her boss. One day I gave Jamie the name of a newly hot literary agent and suggested she have lunch with her and discuss how our magazine could work with some of the writers in this woman's stable. I'd recently had lunch with the agent myself, but since Jamie was directly involved in assigning articles, the contact would be important for her, too.

Originally I'd had a major ulterior motive in meeting with this agent: My fantasy was to write a book one day soon and I felt it would be good to nurture a relationship with a big agent so that when I finally felt the timing was right, I could approach her about representing me. Naturally, I didn't share this self-promoting strategy with Jamie.

Two weeks after Jamie's lunch with the agent, she walked into my office and resigned. "You'll never believe what happened," she gushed breathlessly. She went on to explain that at the lunch with the very hot agent, she'd discussed writers as she was supposed to, but then she'd told the agent about a book idea *she* had. The agent loved the concept and, in two weeks, had gotten her a $50,000 advance.

"That's fantastic," I said in a voice two octaves above normal. At that moment I felt as if I were melting, like the Wicked Witch of the West.

What you have here is a tale of two women who dreamed of being writers: One got her wish that year and one cried in her beer. Was the book idea I'd been noodling over worth $50,000? I'll never know, because I had chosen to stick to my plan. I had decided it was best to wait for the "right moment" to talk to the agent. I'd been afraid it would be inappropriate for me to bring up a personal project at a business lunch. Besides, I didn't really know the agent yet.

Ohhhhhh, but Jamie obviously hadn't felt shackled by any sense of decorum. Sure, she was lunching on the magazine's dime and she barely knew the agent, but she apparently thought, "Here's my opportunity, let me grab it—because there just might not be a next time." Perhaps she gave a little bit of thought to the fact that the agent might consider her brash for asking, but if the book idea was good and the agent could earn a nice chunk of money, "bad" timing wouldn't matter. So Jamie made some small talk, pushed the food around her plate—and pounced.

Here's a wonderful cautionary tale about the dangers of not pouncing. Rita and Barry Aurich met in the Seattle-Tacoma airport. She was on her way back from a business trip to Minneapolis and was waiting for a delayed flight to Yakima, Washington. He was flying back from a vacation in Mexico and was due to board a flight to Eugene, Oregon.

The two began a casual conversation, the kind you might have with anyone sitting next to you when flights are delayed. Though Rita was engaged, she felt instantly attracted to Barry. When his flight was called ten minutes later, he flashed her a smile good-bye—and her heart sank. There had been a real connection—something she didn't feel with her fiancé—and now she was letting him out of her sight. She hadn't gotten his last name and there would be no way to find him.

Fortunately, Barry felt the same connection and the same

panic, and he began to concoct a plan as soon as he got on his plane. He wrote down everything Rita had told him about herself, and the next day he placed the following ad in the Yakima newspaper:

SLEEPLESS SINCE SEATTLE! I left without even getting her name. Please help me find a woman I met at SeaTac airport Tuesday night. She moved back to Yakima a year ago after living in Boston 5 years. She's 32, tall, slender, light brown/blond straight hair, brown eyes, has several dogs & cats, never been married & works in financial planning field. If you know who she is please have her call Barry in Eugene at . . .

A friend of Rita's spotted the ad, made the connection, and, along with Rita's mother, talked her into calling. Rita had not grabbed the opportunity in the airport, but now she was being given a crazy second chance. She didn't make the mistake again. She and Barry were married several months later.

4 Principles of Successful Pouncing

Are you ready to pounce and snatch? Throw out the 3×5 cards and follow these four steps.

1. *Calculate the all-it-takes factor.* Getting what you want will involve effort on your part, there's no way around it. If you want to be a lawyer, you need to go to law school;

if you want to lose twenty pounds, you need to change the way you eat. You must pinpoint *only* those things you need to achieve your goal—and skip all the rest.

One of the observations I've made about women who get what they want is that they're always eliminating the bullshit steps. It's as if they've decorated a room with perfect pieces so they don't have to bother with lots of unnecessary, tacky knickknacks.

I remember the first time I ever saw a woman cut to the chase and get what she wanted. In the last chapter I mentioned that while I was in my twenties and a writer at *Glamour* magazine, I had done volunteer work for a cable TV station. I was semi-serious about pursuing a career in television, and I figured that volunteering would both help me see if I really liked TV and provide me with experience I could use on my résumé. One day when I was returning to my desk at *Glamour,* another writer on staff introduced me to a friend with whom she'd just had lunch.

"Sarah graduated from college a couple of months ago and wants to go into television," my coworker said. "I was telling her about the stuff you do on the side. Maybe you could explain it better than I can."

I did a five-minute show-off routine for the college grad, telling her about the station and how it worked and the great opportunities for someone who didn't have any experience but was eager to learn. I added that if she'd like to call me sometime, I could arrange to meet her and tell her how to go about breaking in there. She thanked me graciously and left.

I didn't hear from her, which surprised me because she

seemed like a ball of fire. But about two weeks later, one of the producers at the cable TV station mentioned a new writer who was volunteering there and it was *her.*

Well, my first reaction was "that little bitch." She'd pumped me for info and then gone behind my back and gotten her foot in the door. But later I thought how smart she'd been. What she needed was simply the name of the place that was using volunteers, and I'd eagerly given it to her that day. She didn't need another meeting with *me.*

How do you determine the steps you need and the ones you can blow off? You must talk to as many people as possible who have gotten *exactly* what you want. I've always been an information gatherer, but over time I've found that I waste a huge amount of time and effort speaking to people on the periphery, people only a little bit in the know on the issue. Those people are always happy to offer insight and advice, but much of what they tell you will be unnecessary, because they don't really know what they're talking about. That's what happened to a friend of mine who was attempting to become pregnant with her second child. She'd conceived her first practically without undressing, but this time she was having no luck. She began confiding in friends, looking for guidance.

"They were wonderfully sympathetic," she says, "and they offered lots of tips, like relax, get massages, and take a weekend trip to a country inn with my husband. They told me, 'You did it the first time, you'll do it again.' But I finally talked to someone who had been through the same thing and she explained that there's something called secondary infertility and she told me to get to a doctor immediately. As it turned out I wasn't ovulating as efficiently as I had been three and a half years before and I needed Clomid. I did appreciate the help of the other women, but the truth is, they were volunteering guidance without really knowing." A common occurrence that can really mess you up and should be avoided at all costs.

2. *Find Waldo.* You've made your all-it-takes list and there's probably a range of activities on it. Now there's some research you must do, some calls you must make. And, of course, there are people you must see, because when it comes to getting what you want in life, it generally involves getting it from someone else. A fascinating phenomenon I've noticed about women who manage to get their cake and eat it, too, is that they determine very quickly who that person is. I call it the "find Waldo" step. There are lots of people in the picture who can be supportive and offer guidance, but someone, somewhere, has the true power to reward you with the prize. It's the person in the company who has the clout to give you the contract, or the right fertility doctor, or the great trainer, or the most dynamic and imaginative real estate agent. You must find the person you need and make contact.

I had lunch the other day with a friend who had decided five years ago that her goal was to become a travel writer so that she could see the world without having to pay for the trips. Since the day she first told me of her dream she has walked across glaciers in Alaska, traveled by barge along the entire length of the Seine, explored the Greek islands, and taken twenty cruises, including a transatlantic trip on the *QE II*. And that, so to speak, is just the tip of the iceberg. When I asked how she'd pulled it off, she said, "It took me awhile to realize that it all comes down to getting to know the publicity people who represent hotels and resorts and cruise lines. In the beginning I concentrated on my writing and learning about the business, but eventually I realized you get the trips because you know the person who can give them to you. I've gone to tons of press events and figured out which people had the power to arrange a trip on the Orient Express or give me a room at the Connaught in London."

There's always a Waldo. You have to ask and snoop and use all the intuitive powers you possess. But you must find him or her, for they hold the golden key.

3. *Seize the moment.* Don't make the mistake I did when I didn't tell the book agent my idea, but the woman who worked for me did. Here's my rule of thumb today: If there is a great opportunity within twenty feet, grab it and worry later about whether you seemed pushy, inappropriate, or overly eager.

I have this very successful friend who is married to a wonderful guy, and it was only lately that she confessed to me how she had met her husband. "At age thirty-five," she says, "I woke up one day and realized that I desperately wanted to be married and have children, and I was going to have to put all my effort into making it happen. So I decided to pursue every single opportunity I could think of. I joined clubs, went on singles' trips, signed up for a share in a summer house with other singles, and left my business card on the tables of strange men in restaurants, even though a year before I would have seen that as totally crass and inappropriate. One day I was talking to a male friend on the phone when we heard his call waiting beep and he put me on hold to see who it was. When he came back, he mentioned the name of the person who'd called, and it happened to be a guy I had met a few times through our circle of friends. I asked him, 'Is he seeing anyone?' It turned out he wasn't and my friend set us up. We got married a year later. If I were doing an ad, the tag line would have to say: I met my husband because of call waiting."

4. *Discover your inner movie star.* To get what you want, you have to feel you deserve it, and, unfortunately, pouncing and snatching don't allow much time for working on your sense of entitlement. Try this shortcut: Go out and buy something absolutely expensive and wonderful to wear, and get a haircut that gives you a whole new look. When you dress and act like a movie star, you often feel like one. It's far less time consuming than listening to forty hours of affirmation tapes.

Little Ways to Get Your Butt Moving

It can be hard to get moving, even when you've figured out the steps you need to take and the people you need to see. You may still feel nervous, uncertain, hesitant, or overwhelmed. Here are a few tricks for getting moving.

• *Jump into the middle.* One reason it's hard to get started is that the first steps are so often excruciatingly tedious or boring. When you're looking for a new job, for instance, step one is invariably "redo résumé," and that's as appealing as "schedule appointment for new dental crown." If you're dreaming about a second honeymoon, your first step may be to "figure out what I can afford"— and boy, is that a downer. So, skip step one and move immediately to step three, which is likely to be more pleasant—like "have lunch with Alison and ask her to explain the company's hierarchy" or "leaf through travel magazines and decide on three possible destinations."

• *Take a road test.* I've noticed that women who get what they want often do a test drive before they fully commit to something. It not only gives them a comfort-level reading, but it also creates momentum.

"There are times when you can dive right into the water and see what happens, but you can also test the water without getting soaked—without making a black or white decision," says Jennifer Kushell, the twenty-five-year-old head of the Young Entrepreneurs Network. "I think that's something women often don't realize they can do. Women plan too much before they say something or before they present an idea. But you're not going to know if you're approaching the mark if you don't test the waters."

I think many of us are reluctant to do this because we feel guilty about wasting someone else's time. You don't want to make someone show you nine condos in Florida, because, though you'd love a winter getaway, you're not certain you can afford one or if Florida's really the right place for you.

Women who get what they want never hesitate this way. I first discovered this when I was applying for a senior editor job at a magazine run by this dazzling editor in chief who not only gets what she wants but seems to get what everyone else wants, too. My initial interview with her went well, and I left her office feeling optimistic. She'd asked me to do a major critique of the magazine, and I assumed that she would only have me undertake such a big project if she considered me a serious contender for the position.

I can still recall the weekend I spent doing the report. There was a heat wave in New York, and instead of heading for the beach, I pored over endless back issues of her magazine dressed only in my underwear. I handed in the critique and then I waited. And waited. I called several times, telling her assistant I was eager to hear back. But I never heard a word.

At the time I thought I must have totally blown the critique. But as I came to know this editor over the years, and saw how she got what she wanted time and time again, I realized that what she'd done that day was give me a road test. In hindsight, I had probably been one of dozens of candidates, not one of two or three finalists. She didn't ask me to do the critique because she thought I was a contender, but to see if I was.

Don't feel guilty about doing a road test. If you put someone through a little effort, it will even out in the end. A road test is what I should have tried with the book agent. Since I felt nervous pitching my idea over lunch, I could have at least tested the waters with a couple of questions: Are you looking for new clients? or Do you mind when magazine editors try to sell you *their* books?

• *Create a deadline you can't miss.* If you're having trouble getting off the dime, it can help to impose a deadline on yourself or even allow someone else to. This will force you to get things done. That's what designer Cynthia Rowley did. She was riding the El (the citywide system of elevated trains) during her student days at the Art Institute of Chicago. One day a buyer for Marshall Fields asked her whose jacket she was wearing. "It's mine," said Rowley, "I'm a designer." Though Rowley had designed the jacket, she wasn't a professional designer—*yet.* The unsuspecting buyer invited Rowley to come by her office the next week and show her line. Rather than admit that she didn't *have* a line, Rowley allowed "next week" to become *her* deadline, the time by which she'd take her first steps as a designer. She spent a harried weekend going to fabric stores and creating five items of clothing to take to the buyer. Although she confessed at the meeting that she wasn't really an active designer, she got her first order: for twelve teal velveteen jackets.

6 Rules You Must Ignore

Once you've decided to ignore the advice that says you must start at the beginning and wait for the right moment, you will be on your merry way. But people will continue to give you unsolicited tips on how you should proceed. Be wary of much of the advice offered, and especially ignore these six pieces of wisdom.

1. Get the Right Training

For some things you do need specialized training, but there are plenty for which you don't. You should not automatically assume you need training simply because it seems "obvious."

A few years ago a woman in the research department came to me and announced that she was leaving to go to graduate school in order to fulfill a longtime dream. I expected her to say she was pursuing a master's in social work so she could counsel people or a degree in environmental science so she could rid the world of garbage. I was dumbfounded when she told me that her secret dream was to be a magazine writer. For several years she had been working at an actual magazine in the midst of dozens of editors, many of whom would have helped her shape an idea and get an article published, but rather than take advantage of such a terrific shortcut, she was going to stay locked into some guideline that she had once been offered and obviously still felt was her best approach.

Men are wonderful at not letting the concept of the "perfect experience" get in their way. There's a well-known anchorman on TV today who seems very experienced. Before this national job he anchored a local newscast. But do you know what he did before that? He hosted infomercials on tooth brighteners. When he was offered the "big" job, do you think he ran around screaming, "I can't, I can't. I've never covered a war. I've never even covered a hurricane. Maybe I should get a degree in broadcast journalism first"? Of course he didn't.

2. Start at the Bottom

Sometimes you really must. But certainly not always. Look for back doors and shortcuts that will allow entry several stories up. Wanda Urbanska, who wrote the beautiful book *Simple Living,* told me a wonderful story once about jumping five steps ahead of where she was supposed to be. "In my senior year in high school, I was writing the community column for this throwaway publication—sort of a shopper—in Brewer, Maine," she says. "My father suggested I try to get an interview with Senator Edmund Muskie for the paper, since they always ran one cover story. Much to my surprise his press secretary said yes. We were in the middle of Watergate, so I asked him, 'Could the country survive an impeachment.' He said yes, he thought the country *could* survive. I began to get the sense that because of answers like this, it was a bigger story. I went by the office of the *Bangor Daily News* and asked to speak to one of the top editors in charge. I told him that I had interviewed Muskie and would like to submit the story to him. He looked at me skeptically and said, 'Well, we *have* a man in Washington.' I told him, 'Well, why don't you take a look at it,' and I took out the article. He started pencil editing it as he read it, so I knew he was going to run it. After they published it, they offered me a chance to write about my town on a regular basis. They assumed I was older because I was tall, and they were shocked when they found out later that I was still in high school, but by then I was already a regular. And that's how I got my start in journalism."

3. Speak to the Right Person

There's the right person to talk to when you want something and then there's the *best* person, and they are not always the same. The best person is the one who can give you the information you seek or help you meet a need, because she has both knowledge and power. The right person is often the one you're told to see because protocol suggests you should go that route. Bending the rules can be valuable.

If at all possible, try to avoid seeing the right person and, like a heat-seeking missile, go directly to the best person.

WARNING: If you go around the right person, you may do some damage. I once held my breath and did this. As a junior writer at *Glamour* I was in charge of writing short items like "The Warning Signs of Vaginitis." I finally decided to try a full-length article. Rather than hand in the piece to an articles editor, "the right person," I put it on the desk of the editor in chief, who read it in ten minutes and announced she loved it. The articles editor was terrific to me, although I think it did dismay her that I made the beeline around her. Still, I felt if I didn't, I'd get stuck. The articles editor tended to ask for extensive rewrites before turning an article over to the editor in chief, and I was afraid if she did that to me, I'd lose my nerve and never finish the piece. It was purely a matter of survival. I ended up repairing the damage by pleading ignorance.

4. Pay Your Dues

This phrase generally means that you must work at or take part in an activity for a certain length of time before you can move on to the next step. One thing I've discovered is that the size of the dues a person calculates must be paid is almost always equal to the size of the dues she paid when she was in the same situation. This kind of person will offer excuses like "You're not quite ready yet." Do anything possible to escape their timetable for you.

5. Strike When the Iron's Hot

It may be much better to strike when it's just heating up.

6. Cool Your Jets

Some people love to slow your speed. They use phrases like "Cool your jets," "Give it time," or "Let's wait and see." Those phrases always strike me as moronic because they leave you in a totally passive state, unable to help things along. When a thirty-seven-year-old friend failed to get pregnant after six months of trying, she consulted her doctor. She knew at her age the window of opportunity was smaller and she didn't want to waste time. The doctor admonished her: "You've got to give it time," he said. "I don't want to hear from you until you've been trying for a year." When she consulted a fertility doctor seven months later, it turned out there was a problem that could have been taken care of earlier. Before you take anyone's advice to "just wait," always ask yourself, What am I waiting for?

I'm sure Jamie, the woman who got a $50,000 advance for her book, had been told on plenty of occasions to cool her jets, but she was flying fast, straight, and high. Through trial and error she probably discovered that if you cool your jets, you don't go anywhere.

4

WEAR YOUR HEART
ON YOUR SLEEVE

When I was a junior-level magazine editor in my
twenties, I was pretty far removed from the real
action and politics of the industry, but one time,
quite by accident, I found myself backstage in a drama
about who would become the new editor in chief of one of
the top women's magazines. And it taught me one of the
best lessons I've ever learned.

It all began at lunch one day. I was meeting a woman—
let's call her A—whom I'd once worked with. Though she
was now an executive editor at a magazine, and thus way
out of my league, she would occasionally take me to lunch,
offer me career advice, and provide some distracted men-
toring. On this particular day A arrived out of breath. It
had been a crazy week, she said, she had so much going
on, and though I think she planned to leave it at that, her
excitement got the better of her, and she made a surprising

confession. The day before she had been offered the position of editor of one of the most prestigious women's magazines. The previous editor, who had been in the job for well over a decade, had just been sent on her way—to discover life as a consultant. A was thrilled, of course, but she hadn't said yes just yet. She had been considering a move to L.A. and taking the job would throw a wrench in her plans. She had told them she needed time to think, to be sure. Under normal circumstances, she probably would never have shared this information with me—I just happened to be in her path during this crazy week.

There were two things that occurred to me after we parted. One, how great it was to be privy to such juicy news. And second, how cool and collected A was. She was handling everything with such equanimity. I remember thinking that the people who made the job offer must have been impressed.

About two weeks later there were new developments and again, almost by accident, I learned all about them. I was standing in the hallway outside my office one afternoon when B, a magazine editor and the girlfriend of one of the top editors at the magazine where I worked, dashed by, absolutely in a tizzy. Since we knew each other casually, I said hi, and told her that her boyfriend, whom she was obviously hoping to talk to, was still out to lunch. Fearful, I suppose, of bursting at the seams, she pulled me into my office and said that she'd just had an interview for a fantastic job—the editor in chief position at the very same magazine that was courting A. B said that she knew she was a long shot for the job—she was only a senior articles editor—but she thought the interview had gone fantastically well.

I couldn't believe that I knew two women up for the same big job, though I was slightly confused. A had indicated that the job had been offered to her. Did this mean she had turned it down? I didn't breathe a word about A but listened to B describe the interview.

She looked adorable, by the way, in this incredible neon yellow silk blouse and baggy pants that would have been the last thing I'd have grabbed for a job interview, and yet the whole effect was very hip. She told me that she'd been so excited during her meeting with the head guy that she had gushed instead of talked, that she had poured out dozens of ideas, and that she had barely been able to stay seated. In fact, at one point she *hadn't* stayed seated. When she had been describing how much better the covers might look with some of the model's body showing rather than just the face, she had jumped up off her chair and demonstrated. I was bug-eyed watching her and listening to her talk. Part of me thought she sounded fabulous and the other part wondered if the guy had sat there thinking she must be a wacko.

Then her boyfriend appeared in my doorway and she was gone, making me swear not to reveal any of this to a soul.

A few days later the word was out all through the industry. B had gotten the job. The one thing I still wasn't certain about was A—why had she decided to blow off such a great opportunity. Eventually I heard through the rumor mill that A hadn't turned down the job at all. Apparently, during the days that she was coolly considering her options, someone had suggested to the president that he meet with one more candidate. That was B, and B had stolen the job right out from under A.

Over the next weeks, all sorts of editors I knew were asking, How did she do it—she's so young? And I knew. Instead of being cool and calculating, she had been passionate and intense and dazzling. She had shown how much she really, really wanted the job. She had even jumped out of her seat, and *that* was one of the best lessons I ever learned.

In the last chapter I talked about how important it is, when you're just getting started, to determine who the people are who can give you, at the very least, helpful information or advice and, at the most, the thing you want. Have you figured out who they are yet? Well, it's these people who need to see just how eager you are. You've heard that old expression, "Don't wear your heart on your sleeve"? Well, if you're going to get what you want, you must take that little heart of yours, put it on your sleeve, and let people see it passionately pumping away.

Now, I know you're reading this strategy and thinking that it's bad advice. Certainly it contradicts much of what you've been told. If you're like me, you grew up hearing people warn you not to get carried away, not to let your emotions get the best of you, not to be an open book, and certainly not to let them see you cry or sweat.

And the evidence, at first glance, supports this advice. Just look at women who get what they want—they seem to be such *cool customers.* At the opposite end of the spectrum are the Sean Youngs of the world. Remember when she wanted the part of Cat Woman in *Batman* and went on all those television shows dressed in that ridiculous cat costume and mask. Her campaign not only didn't win her the part, it made her seem desperate, as volatile as a cougar and even a little nutty.

Well, you don't want to model yourself after Sean Young, but you do need to let them see how much you want something. As I've gone after more and more in life, I've come to see that wearing my heart on my sleeve has actually been spectacularly effective for me. Revealing your passion rather than concealing it is the best way to win big prizes. When director Alan Parker was casting the part of Evita, Madonna was not at all ashamed to show that she wanted it in a bad, bad way. She sent the director a four-page handwritten letter. "I can't remember what was in the letter," she says. "All I know is that I begged and pleaded with Alan. I promised him that I would give him my all, and that I wouldn't disappoint him. I wanted him to know that I wouldn't be a spoiled brat." She also compared her own experience to Evita's, showed how much they were alike, and thus why she could play the dictator's wife so beautifully.

Women who get what they want may appear to be cool as cucumbers in public, but I guarantee you that when they meet up with the person who has the power to give them what they want, they don't hold back. They gush, they're exuberant, they show all the fire of a hot tamale.

Why It Pays to Be a Hot Tamale

I know you're worried that someone will think you're coming on too strong and that you may need to be avoided at all costs. But here are just four reasons why being a hot tamale won't get you burned.

1. By being passionate, you demonstrate with certainty what it is you need. You'd be surprised, but unless you get carried away, people often aren't sure that you crave something they're in a position to facilitate. They're busy, preoccupied, and don't notice—or they mistake that look on your face for something else entirely, like worry or indigestion. Judy George, the CEO and chairman of the board of Domain Home Fashions, a multimillion-dollar business that she founded, calls showing your passion "turning on your high beams." That's a great analogy because what you're doing is shedding light on the intensity of your interest, letting the right person see clearly what you have on your mind.

2. By being passionate, you give the other person the impression that there might be something in it for *her.* When you're that passionate about obtaining something, it suggests that you feel a major commitment to it, which in many cases could produce a nice dividend for the person doing the giving. They assume you'll work your butt off if you want something so badly, or, at the very least, be eternally grateful. There's another successful write-the-director-a-letter story that illustrates this point. When director Gus

Van Sant was casting the part of Suzanne Stone, the murderous would-be anchorwoman in *To Die For*, Nicole Kidman wasn't on his short list. He was hoping for Meg Ryan or another proven star. So Kidman got his home number and called him. She told him that she felt destined to play the part and that she admired his work. After that conversation he gave her a screen test and then went on to cast her in the role. He later said that he figured anyone who wanted the part that badly would put her all into it. And she did. Kidman got fabulous reviews, and even won a Golden Globe nomination.

3. By being passionate, you encourage the other person to connect with you personally. That connection can make him feel loyal to you and invested in you.

Earlier I mentioned a dynamic and super-successful trial lawyer named Suzelle Smith, whom *Redbook* interviewed for an article on the bold new breed of women attorneys. I had the chance to talk to her then about her work. As half of the Los Angeles firm of Howarth & Smith, she wins multimillion-dollar settlements for her clients, in part, she says, by showing the jury her passion for the case and her personal investment in it. "I wouldn't take a case if I didn't believe in it," says Smith, "and when I come into the courtroom, I put my heart into it. When I'm involved, the jury knows that it's personal. Jurors are looking for characteristics they can relate to when they're judging a trial. You have to have the courage to expose yourself. The jurors know that if they decide against my client, it will be bad for him *and* bad for me."

I'm convinced that I'm living in my fabulous house

because I wore my heart on my sleeve for the people sell-ing it. As I mentioned earlier, when my husband and I stum-bled on this town house it was love at first sight. There were lots of wonderful nooks and crannies and a garden out back and a room that could be my study—we were smit-ten. We wanted it, and we felt we'd be heartbroken if we didn't get it.

Unfortunately, there were some major obstacles. The real estate market had recently picked up, and our agent learned that several other couples had already been back to see the house a second time. The day after we saw the house we made a verbal offer over the phone, and then we had to wait several days for the inspection before we could make a formal offer. I was so nervous I could barely sleep the weekend before the inspection—what if someone else made a better offer? After breakfast on Saturday I sug-gested to my husband that we walk by the house so that our kids, who hadn't seen it, could get a look at the out-side. But I had another motive. For some strange reason I felt there was a chance we'd bump into the owners (whom we hadn't met), and there might be an opportunity to form a connection.

Our timing was just a little off. As we were heading up the block, about ten yards from the house, we saw a woman carrying groceries up the front steps. Gone was our opportunity to just "bump" into her. So I did something that mortified my husband and kids. I hollered out, "Hello." When the woman turned around, I waved and called out to her, "We looked at your house yesterday and we loved it."

"Oh, wonderful," she said. "Would you like to come in and take another look?"

It was a great experience. As our kids ran up and down the stairs, my husband and I had a chance to talk to the couple about everything from storm gutters to raising children in New York City. They told us they were moving because their last child was headed for college. They said we reminded them of themselves when they'd moved in fifteen years earlier.

Our real estate agent called us later and said the couple had reported to their agent that they wanted very much to sell us the house.

Okay, I'm not a fool, and I know they would have jumped at some buyer offering thousands more, but I also know that because they liked us and appreciated our delight in the house, they were open to our concerns, patient when the inspection had to be redone, and even told us they'd finance a second mortgage if we needed it. That loud "Hello" and the flailing of the arms had paid off for me.

A friend of mine, Jeffry Culbreth, who is the talent executive for the "Rosie O'Donnell Show," says that in her fifteen or so years as a booker for a variety of shows, including "Today," she has been unabashed when it comes to making a personal connection with celebrity publicists and showing how badly she wants a particular star for the show. "I try to form a personal connection with everyone I can," she says, "and it's sincere. I'm really interested in people. I ask about their kids, I use my southern charm, I flirt. And if they're about to tell me no, I really use that personal connection. I say, 'Darlin', you *can't* do this to me. We go way back,' and that makes it harder for them to say no. When I was booking the 'Today' show I was sure there were a few people who thought, 'I can't tell Jeffry no. She works on a top floor at Rockefeller Center and she might *jump*.'"

4. By being passionate, you make the other person long to be around you. As they say, we're all voyeurs at heart, and being in the same room with lots of passion can be delicious, contagious. Recently I had the chance to talk to Jennifer Kushell, the head of the Young Entrepreneurs Network, who has been creating her own businesses since she was fourteen and just wrote a book on how to start your own business. Her exuberance is a joy to be around and it's paid off for her.

"I actually got a talking-to not that long ago from my aunt who owns a company," says Kushell, "and she said, 'You know, you've got to be calmer when you're talking to people. You get so excited and you raise your voice and you're leaning forward. You've got to calm down because people are going to think you're too young and inexperienced.' But I think enthusiasm is definitely, definitely something people like. If you're dealing with a huge bank or a big sponsor or a bunch of bureaucrats, you probably need to scale back, but when you're dealing with people one-on-one, people you want to build relationships with, you've got to be excited. If you're not, you're going to keep everything at a very low energy level. It's just like when you're doing any kind of public speaking, if you're not smiling, no one else will be. When you show your excitement, you end up giving people an *energy transfer*."

Washington's Betsy Myers agrees: "I'm passionate, and it works for me. People find it refreshing. People may not like you, but they respect your commitment—they're drawn to it. They say things like, 'she *loves* what she's doing,' and they assume it will turn out well."

12 Things You Shouldn't Hesitate to Do When You're Hot for Something

You can express your passion in words, but sometimes *action* is called for. That action may feel slightly awkward to you or even extreme, but don't let that stop you. Kathy Bishop, woman's editor of the *New York Post,* told me that several years ago, when she was just starting out, she decided she really wanted a job with the magazine *Harper's Bazaar* but wasn't sure how to proceed, since the new editor in chief, Liz Tilberis, was still in London, wrapping up her final duties at British *Vogue* and getting ready to head to America. Bishop turned to a male mentor for advice.

"He told me to get on a plane, fly to London, and take Liz to tea," Bishop says. "It took me a minute to realize he was absolutely serious. It was such an over-the-top thing to do, but that's what he thought the situation called for. Since then I've come to see that a bold move like that is something some men wouldn't think twice about but a woman considers drastic. I took his advice. In the end, I went to Paris for the appointment—Liz was there for the fashion shows—and I got the job."

If you want something, you may very well have to:

1. Send a handwritten note expressing your desire—on the best notecard stock available (avoid anything that bends easily or has flowers or squirrels on it).
2. Write a more formal but very individualized cover letter describing how strongly you feel about what it is you want.
3. Call the person, even if it's really, really hard to do.
4. Ask someone you know to make an introduction, even if you dread asking them to do so. (You can be sure someone has done the same for them on another occasion.)
5. Dress to the nines for any kind of meeting or get-together, even if it means buying a brand-new outfit (and fantastic shoes!) the day before.
6. Introduce yourself to total strangers at a party or an event. It can change your life.
7. Pull an all-nighter to get done anything that needs to be done.
8. Do something on very short notice.
9. Buy someone a great meal.
10. Call the maître d' of the restaurant where you plan to have that great meal and explain how important the event is and how you would like him to take good care of you (and then tip him $20).
11. Get on a plane and go after what you want, even on your own dime.
12. Use expressions like "This is fantastic," "I've never been so excited," and "I've never wanted anything so much."

When Good Old Passion Isn't Enough

Gushing can be good, but often you have to take your passion one step further. When you are talking to someone who has information or resources you need, there comes a point at which you may have to form your raw enthusiasm into a request of some kind. Because even though the other person knows you're interested, he may not realize specifically what you want and specifically when you need it. You have to ask.

In one of my jobs as editor in chief of a magazine, I agreed to work with a book publishing company on several books that would carry the magazine's name. In a staff meeting I asked editors to submit the names of any regular contributors to the magazine who might be good for one of the projects. I suggested that they could also include their own names on the list, and several nodded in appreciation. Over the next weeks, these editors each sent me a short list of names—a few included their own—which I turned over to the publisher, who was going to screen the writers and determine who was best for each of the books. Several weeks later, the book editor in charge sent me a proposal from the writer who'd been picked for the health book, a woman who had written for the magazine on numerous occasions. I learned later that the screening process hadn't been particularly methodical. When the book editor had connected with one writer who sounded good, she'd asked her to submit a proposal, even though she hadn't spoken to everyone on the list.

Well, before long one of my editors called me to tell me how disappointed she was that she hadn't been given an opportunity to work on the health book. As it turned out, the book publisher had called her once, asked for some clips, but then never followed up. She really wanted to write the book, she told me, and she thought she'd made that clear by putting her name on the list.

Her approach couldn't have been worse.

Sure, she'd expressed some interest. She'd smiled when I said I was open to having a staffer take on the project, and she'd put her name in the hat. But that just wasn't enough. Her lackluster behavior made me assume that she'd be willing to do the book but not that she wanted the job with all her heart.

Here's what she *should* have done.

After the meeting, she should have popped into my office and said, "I really appreciate your giving the editors here a shot at the project. I would absolutely kill for the opportunity to write the health book. Would you consider submitting only my name for that project? I promise to do a great job for you."

And what if I'd said, "I'm happy to submit your name, but they want a bunch of writers to choose from, so I need to send a whole list over"?

She should have gotten the name of the book editor, called her up and said: "You'll notice that my name is on the list of writers, and I wanted to let you know how much I'd love to do the book. I'm going to send over some clips of articles I wrote that will show how my writing style fits perfectly with this project. Could I meet with you to talk about the project and my ideas for getting started?"

Considering that the book editor appeared to be taking the path of least resistance on the project, this might have been all my editor had to do to secure the prize.

In life, it's not enough just to put your name on the list. You must come right out and ask for what you want.

Now, by no means is that an easy job. It's one thing to stand in a room and gush about what you love and why it's the best thing in the world. It's quite another to pause and then ask for money or information or help.

I hate to ask for anything. I used to assume that just asking for something was difficult—forming the words and letting them squeak out of my mouth—but when I was raising money for my kids' school, I found it to be quite fun. Suddenly I realized that it isn't asking per se that's a problem for me, but rather requesting something for *myself.* I guess I find it a little bit like that scene in the musical *Oliver,* where our hero has just finished his first meal in the orphanage. He goes up to the dreaded man in black with his porridge bowl and asks, "More, sir, may I please have some more?" The child is practically banished to hell. When you come right out and ask for something, there is the fear that not only will you be denied what you want, but you'll also be laughed at, humiliated, or run out of town.

First, let me reassure you, that rarely happens. If you ask for something in the right way, the other person generally finds it impressive, even if he isn't prepared to give you everything you want. You will not be thrown out on your butt. But let me repeat: You must ask in the *right* way. Just presenting your request succinctly and with lots of nerve won't necessarily do you any good. Oh, it may work fine if the request is a simple one or they were planning to give it to you anyway, but if you're asking for something that is hard to give or not what they'd ever expect little ol' you to want, then you have to take a very special approach.

Before you open your mouth to ask for anything, proceed to the next section.

The Simple but Amazing Little Secret to Getting People to Give You What You Want

Over the years I've read several good books on sales skills and I've watched plenty of great people on the sales side of magazines in action. All in all I've been exposed to lots of selling techniques, but as far as I'm concerned, there's one little trick that works better than all the others. You must determine what the TPB will be for the person who has something you want.

What the heck is a TPB? It's the acronym for a phrase used by a woman I know who is stunningly brilliant at persuading people to spend money with her company. It stands for Their Personal Bonus, and what she means is that you must enable the other person to see what bonus they will collect when they've given you what you want. If you don't do this, if you make the request all about *you* and what's necessary to make *you* happy, your chances of success will be extremely low.

96

This sounds obvious, but many of us get so caught up in our excitement or nervousness that we don't get around to addressing the other person's needs or revealing what's in it for him or her. I also think women sometimes take the advice about the importance of talking up their accomplishments and go about it the wrong way. I'll never forget a particularly irritating memo I got from a woman asking for a raise. It was all "me, me, me," and "I did this" and "I did that," and she even used the phrase "I'm coming off a particularly strong first quarter," which sounded like something you'd say at a commodities firm, not a magazine. There was nothing about how much she'd enjoyed working at the magazine or what great ideas she planned to submit in the future. Her memo left me feeling less than generous. She had neglected to find TPB.

I used to absolutely stink when it came to getting beyond my own interests while asking for something. I'll tell you one humiliating example because it illustrates my point so well. When I was a twenty-five-year-old feature writer working at *Glamour*, I walked into the office of the editor in chief, Ruth Whitney, to ask for something I wanted beyond belief. It had recently been announced that a group of scientists was planning to explore the depths of Loch Ness with newly developed sonar equipment, hoping to finally prove or disprove whether there was a monster lumbering along the bottom. In my enthusiasm, I had arranged to stay at the same inn in Northern Scotland where the scientists would be camped out so that I could interview them about their experiences. I had this fabulous vision of myself in front of a blazing fire or walking the windswept paths

97

with sixteen male scientists nipping at my heels. I begged Ruth Whitney to let me write an article about this experience and to pick up the bill for the trip.

Well, none of this seemed to appeal to her. She kept arguing that it would be awfully expensive and that with *Glamour*'s three-month lead time, any news from the expedition would be old news by the time my article came out.

"What's the twist that would make the article work for *Glamour*?" she asked in exasperation (the kind of exasperation that should have caused me to turn on my heels right then and there). "I don't see it."

I stood there for a moment in her office, desperately trying to cough up something. Finally, I had it: "What if I *sleep* with the Loch Ness monster?"

At that point I think she was ready to call security, so I fled her office without waiting for a reply.

I think that was the pinnacle of bad asking. I had made my request totally about me. If I had given it some thought, there might really have been a twist that would have made the article right for *Glamour*—or for the editor. Who knows? Maybe she would have loved a set of bagpipes.

How to Find Their Personal Bonus

How do you determine TPB? Sometimes it's obvious. In other cases, you're going to have to think a little harder, maybe even do some detective work. Consider what the other person is going through, what pressure she's under, what needs she may have. Your offer has to be something that she views as valuable and you have to make her worry that she'll experience regret if she passes it up. One of the other observations director Gus Van Sant made about Nicole Kidman's approach to asking for the part was that it was exactly the kind of no-holds-barred behavior that the character would have engaged in.

If, for instance, you are making a career shift and asking someone to hire you for a job in a different field, it may be tough for him to see any obvious bonus. You appear game and fabulously passionate, but he's going to have to spend time teaching, training, bringing you up to speed, and may end up with several ticked-off staff members in the process. What can you offer that might make all that training and those headaches worth it to him? Maybe it's a Rolodex of names, or experience in setting up a website, or expertise in marketing that could be applied very effectively to *his* business. Don't let him guess it. Spell out the bonus that will be placed in his hands during the weeks after he's picked you. I once hired a fabulous editor who came not from another magazine, which is usually the case, but from a company that forecasts trends. She didn't have a pool of hot writers, which you usually hope for with an editor, but she made up for it with her insight about consumers and trends. The bonus was tantalizing to me.

Back for a moment to the person on my staff who wanted to write the book: I explained what she should have said to the editor but I left out one important part— TPB. As I said, she should have called the book editor, but she should have also pumped the editor for information about what it was she was looking for—maybe the editor needed someone who could write the book quickly, before she left for maternity leave, for example. With that information, the editor could have presented the bonus. ("I'm extremely organized and quick and I can get this book done in six months.")

If you're asking for something in a non-work-related setting, do not underestimate the value of bonuses that are just plain thrilling—or fun—or fattening. Remember when President Clinton ran into criticism for rewarding his campaign donors? Documents revealed that he personally approved a plan under which the Democratic party rewarded some top donors and fund-raisers with meals, coffees, golf outings, and morning jogs with him. The Democratic finance chairman said all of these would "energize" the donors for the next campaign. But that's not all that got offered. In addition to approving these perks, Clinton added one of his own. He would allow key donors to spend a night in the Lincoln bedroom.

Forget for a moment any ethical issues tied to giving away a night in the Lincoln bedroom. What a brilliant TPB. I was invited once to a luncheon Mrs. Clinton gave for female journalists at the White House, and all of us were given about forty-five minutes to tour the second floor before the meal. It was the most wonderful experience. I've never spent the night in the Lincoln bedroom, but I've walked around in there and felt the mattress and I can imagine how fantastic it would be to crawl under those covers for a night. Making someone feel wonderfully special can be a perfect TPB. Of course, you don't want to offer a bonus that will later backfire, like the Lincoln bedroom. But let that at least inspire you to think big—and creatively.

Another point: You may have to offer a bonus even if you don't feel the person deserves one. If you are asking your husband to help more around the house, it may hardly seem like something he should get a bonus for. But regardless, you need a motivator. Let him know how much it will mean to you and how much less of a nag it will make you and how it will give the two of you more quality time together.

The Little Trick That Works in Stubborn Cases

In certain instances, it may be almost impossible to find a specific TPB you can use. Fortunately, there's a universal one that people respond to beautifully: making them feel *important* for saying yes.

My husband, who is a TV newscaster, told me a very funny story recently. He used to anchor the news in Tulsa, Oklahoma, and every night the station he worked for would include a story in their newscast on something that had happened in Oklahoma City, which they received on tape from their sister station in that city (and the Oklahoma City station ran a tape from Tulsa). This was before satellite technology was available, and you won't believe how the tapes were exchanged between the two cities, seventy-five miles apart. One of the reporters or producers from the Tulsa station would go to the token booth at the turnpike and ask drivers going to Oklahoma City if they'd be willing to drop off the tape at the tollbooth there, where someone would pick it up. Not only would they always find a willing messenger, but, according to my husband, no one ever neglected to drop off the tape. In fact, one guy who did forget to leave the tape drove all the way back from Amarillo. "That's amazing," I remarked when he told me this story. "Why do you think people took it so seriously?" He laughed. "Because we had a large sticker that we put on each tape that said, 'URGENT. DATED NEWS MATERIAL. USELESS IF DELAYED.'"

People love to feel that they're part of something that's urgent and portentous, and if you want to motivate them to go along, it helps to create a sense of urgency and importance. Give them the sense that if they help you, it's the next best thing to saving the ozone layer.

Let's say, for instance, that your son's guidance counselor is not giving him much attention, and for good reason—your son covers up his nervousness and uncertainty by acting sullen. What you want is to convince this guy to take more of an interest. You don't know the guidance counselor well enough to determine what bonus might work for him. So use the importance factor. Say something like "I've seen the way you work with kids and it's terrific. You've really helped to shape the futures of some of these kids. My son is at a critical point in his life right now and you could play such an important role in helping to send him in the right direction. If you could help us, I'll work with you and support your efforts. It would mean the world to me."

When You Need Backup

When you are in the process of convincing someone to give you something, it may be necessary to offer proof, backup as to why they would be making a good choice. In fact, even if they don't ask, it's good to offer it anyway.

And, of course, you want whatever you put together to be as thorough and complete as possible. If it's numbers, they must all add up. If it's research, it's got to make sense.

It's also got to look good. Jennifer Kushell says that in her work with beginning entrepreneurs, she's shocked at the unprofessionalism of some of the presentation materials she sees. If anything about your backup material makes you the least bit uncomfortable, it means it's not good enough—and you need to make it better.

Those are pretty obvious suggestions. But there are two not so obvious ones that I've stolen from women who get what they want.

First, keep it short and sweet. If you've done lots of work, you may be tempted to lay it all out there—the charts, the graphs, the newspaper clippings, the personal endorsements, whatever. In many respects, females would make the best Boy Scouts, because we take the "Be prepared" concept so seriously. But what you really want to aim for is the nutshell approach. What is the proof the other person is looking for and how can you sum it up in the absolute simplest way? People are short on time and attention, and if you can succinctly present the reasons you deserve something, it will have a far better impact than if you overload them.

When Judy George was pitching the idea for her furniture company to venture capitalists, she decided not to overwhelm them but to let one picture tell the whole story. "I put some textures and fabrics and paint chips and pictures together," she says. "It reflected a whole different lifestyle and I called it 'The Romance of Life.' It was easy for them to understand and very effective."

Carolyn Maloney, the dynamic Democratic congresswoman from New York City, says that her victory in her first congressional race was the result of presenting voters with one simple but powerful concept. At the time of the race, Maloney, a former and highly acclaimed City Council member, was a Democrat running in a predominantly Democratic district, but her opponent, the Republican incumbent, was liberal and had backed many issues Democrats liked—and as a result was very popular. She was very much a long shot and she needed an idea voters could quickly grab hold of.

"My opponent kept making the point to voters," says Maloney, "that he would be better for the city than me— even as a member of the minority party in Congress— because he was on the powerful appropriations committee. So, here's the question I asked voters over and over again: Who needs him on the appropriations committee representing New York City when *they* voted to cut aid for the city by 62 percent? I mean period, that's it. He was voting his party, the Republican party, and not the city."

When I was up for the job as editor of *Redbook,* I had

several interviews with the president of the magazine division and I knew I needed to write him a strong follow-up note—my backup. He was a charming guy who obviously loved irreverence and my gut told me a formal "Let me review my strengths" letter would be all wrong. During the interview we'd spoken briefly about Julia Roberts, who'd just been photographed for the cover of one of the company's magazines, and I'd remarked that she might be getting a divorce from Lyle Lovett.

"I don't think so," he said. "I hear they're pretty happy."

So instead of a formal note, I simply sent him a picture from one of the tabloids of Lyle and another woman leaving a hotel. It was an irreverent touch I thought he'd like.

The second suggestion is never apologize about your backup. I sat in a meeting once in which a woman talked about a new product she was hoping to launch soon—if she could get backing. When people indicated that the materials she'd provided didn't offer a full enough description, she immediately started with a mea culpa. "Oh, I probably should have put everything in there, but I was trying to be concise . . ." and so on. Don't do that. Simply say you'll get back with whatever is needed.

Why a Bribe Is Nice and Perfectly Legal

A bribe is different than a TPB. The TPB is the big payoff they are going to get from giving you what you want. The bribe is just a little candy, which helps make the whole process more pleasant. When Diane Keaton was up for the lead in *Marvin's Room,* which later earned her an Academy Award nomination, she vowed to try a different approach for her. "I've always felt if you don't let people know you want something, it'll come to you," she said, "which of course is stupid, yet I always lived by that rule. But this time, I thought, 'C'mon, you want it so go for it. You're probably not going to get it anyway, so who cares.'" She says she sent the studio chief cartons of cigarettes and Diet Coke every day for a month.

Do not underestimate flowers, muffins, shoulder rubs (to spouses you are trying to convince), invitations, and fantastic meals.

How Not to Look Scary

How do you come on strong but not too strong? How do you gush without making them blush? How do you avoid looking like Sean Young?

It's essential to pick up any early clues that it's just not working. If they're squirming, back off and allow for some breathing room. It also helps to keep your sense of humor. Don't take everything too seriously. This past year I had the chance to meet Stephanie Denham. After she lost her fifteen-year-old daughter to a drunk driver, Mrs. Denham got involved in her local chapter of MADD—Mothers Against Drunk Driving—and eventually became president of the Mississippi state chapter, helping to revitalize it. She's passionate about her cause, but she told me that because it's such a tragic, disturbing topic, she's learned that it is helpful, when talking to victims' groups or legislative groups that she hopes to persuade about legislation, to use humor to make people more comfortable. "In my presentations, I talk about my daughter, of course, but early on I'll mention that she was remarkably smart and that my husband and I still can't figure out where she came from— I struggled for every grade. This always makes people laugh, and then they can relax."

When It's Time to Undersell

I've spent a lot of time singing the praises of going after things at full throttle, and on most occasions it works. But not always. In some instances, exuberance isn't appropriate, and in some it just plain scares or offends the person you're talking to. Jeffry Culbreth, the booker for the "Rosie O'Donnell Show," loves to start phone conversations with "Hi, girlfriend" or "Hi, boyfriend," delivered in her great Alabama drawl. It warms up almost everyone. However, one time when she placed a call to a big shot and gave him the line, he nearly bit her head off. "Don't ever call me your boyfriend," he snapped. "I am not your boyfriend." She almost died of embarrassment.

Should she cut out all the girlfriend stuff? No, because that girlfriend charm and exuberance is what helps her land the big stars. Occasionally you can wear your heart on your sleeve in a situation in which it seems perfectly appropriate yet it just plain backfires. You don't know until it's too late that the person you're dealing with doesn't appreciate raw passion and exuberance.

There are some situations when it's wise to proceed cautiously and check your passion at the door. Because of the nature of a particular situation, passion may work against you. In the end, you can always go back to get it. Keep your cool with the following people.

- Bankers, backers, and other kinds of moneylenders (they tend to be anxious and may mistake your passion for recklessness). Says Judy George: "My major success is raising money and creating a connection with the customer. I mean, when I go to a store, my passion and my soul are out there. One of my problems, though, in dealing with venture capitalists used to be that I tended to get too excited. It took years of rejection for me to realize that the best way for me to get what I needed for the company was to undersell and overdeliver—yet still have that passion for the business.

- Corporate lawyers.

- People doing the hiring in stodgy companies.

- Groups of people whom you need to win over but who view you as an outsider. I've always noticed that in a group setting, too much passion on the part of someone brand new can make the group squirm. If you are the new department head or a new committee member in the PTA, avoid gushing in front of the group. Instead, divide and conquer. Meet with people individually to win them over.

- On the romantic side, a guy you've flipped for who isn't at that point yet. As someone once said, guys who suspect you're too eager tend to leave skid marks.

So what do you do with these types? Avoid the full frontal attack, which will make them nervous, and instead sneak in from the side. Instead of letting them see how passionate you are for what they could offer you, let them see your passion for what you do: your project, your work, your life. One day, shortly before I got married, I ran down to a little museum in SoHo before dinner with my husband-to-be because I wanted to see an exhibit they were having. I only had forty-five minutes before closing time, but I dashed around, taking it all in. Just as I was leaving, a drop-dead good-looking guy came up to me, smiled, and asked if I'd like to have a cup of coffee with him. I refused politely and on the way out said to myself, "Where was he all those years I went to museums hoping to meet a cute guy?" I knew the answer, of course. What had sent this guy in my direction wasn't the fact that I was a single girl in the museum, but that I was a girl in love with all the things she was seeing.

If you've gushed and pleaded and bribed to no avail, proceed directly to the next chapter.

5

BE TOO BIG FOR YOUR BRITCHES

If you show your passion, if you dare to ask, I guarantee you'll get what you want—much of the time. But, unfortunately, not all of the time. There will be occasions when no matter how eloquently you describe your goal and present your case, they will say no, no, no—and they may even do it with an obnoxious expression on their faces. Or maybe you know up front that a simple request just isn't going to work, that the situation calls for something big and bold, but you have no idea where to start.

This is the point at which it's so easy to feel a surge of disappointment or downright panic, or at the very least resign yourself to not getting what you have your heart set on. But there's another way to look at this kind of moment: This is when the fun begins. Okay, fun may not be quite the right word. But rather than crawl into their beds and decide never to get out again, this is when the women who get what they want rub their hands together and use their imaginations to come up with plan B or maybe even plan Z. Remember the part in *Gone with the Wind* when Scarlett is living with her sisters in the smoldering wreck of Tara and she realizes she must get to Atlanta and convince someone to give her some cash but she has nothing to wear but rags. As she's pondering what to do, her eyes fall upon the green velvet curtains still hanging at the window, one of the few things those horrible Yankees have spared. She begins tearing them off their rods. In the next scene she's sashaying through the streets of Atlanta in a green velvet dress.

When you've asked and they have said no, when you can't even get in to see them, when there doesn't appear to be a simple solution, when there doesn't appear to be any solution *at all,* that's when you must glance around the room and let the curtains inspire you. You have to try something unexpected, bold, over the top, perhaps even wicked—and you'll just have to ignore anyone who claims you are overstepping your bounds or have gotten too big for your britches.

Recently I had the chance to speak to Suzy Kellett, director of the Washington State Film Office. Not only does she have a fabulous job convincing movie companies to make films in her state (she helps lure movies like *The Postman* with Kevin Costner), she is the mother of twenty-four-year-old quadruplets. They are all college graduates and terrific kids. What's especially amazing about this accomplishment is that when her children were ten months old, her husband walked out on her and the kids, and she was forced to raise them as a single parent.

It was a horrible time for her when he first peeled out of there. How did she do it? In part, she says, by using some advice her mother gave her when she was younger: There's more than one way to skin a cat.

Each time Suzy Kellett would run into some obstacle that seemed bigger and stronger and tougher than she was, and the standard way of confronting it just wasn't working, she would do as her mother taught her and devise some ingenious way to handle it.

There's almost always another way to skin the cat, to find something to wear to Atlanta, to pull off what you need to do—you're just going to have to look around and find it.

I'm still experiencing the ramifications from an afternoon eleven years ago when I overstepped my bounds in one of the most creative ways I'd ever done.

It all began when a friend called to tell me she'd met a guy who she thought would be a terrific date for me. She'd moved to New York City several weeks earlier to take a job as a reporter and anchor for a news broadcast on a New York City channel, after working in television in Baltimore, and this was her first day at work. I rarely had time in my single days to watch local news, but because she'd be anchoring, I had planned to be glued to the set that night.

"You're thinking of my social life on your first day at work?" I exclaimed.

"I couldn't help it," she said. "When I met this guy, all I could think was that he'd be perfect for you."

"What's he like?"

"He's my coanchor. You'll see him tonight."

I ate my dinner in front of the tube that night. It was hard to tell just by looking whether this guy had any potential as a soulmate, but he was awfully cute, and he also seemed *normal*. The next day, after telling my friend how fabulous she was on TV, I said, yes, go ahead, please fix me up with him. She'd heard around the newsroom that he'd just broken up with someone and was therefore available, so she gave him my number and got him to swear that he'd call. I waited . . . and waited. It soon became clear that this guy was not going to act on the recommendation of a coworker he'd known for about fourteen seconds.

I suppose I could have responded by giving a sigh of resignation and throwing a wadded-up potato chip bag at the guy's face on the screen, but I really, really liked what I saw and didn't want to give up. So I hatched a little scheme.

At the time, I was the executive editor in charge of articles for *Mademoiselle* magazine, overseeing the editors who assigned and edited the features and columns in the magazine. We had recently begun doing more and more pictorial articles, and that month we were putting together a story called "The Ten Most Eligible Men in America," a mix of famous young single guys like Don Johnson and some cute up-and-coming ones. I picked up my phone one afternoon and told the editor working on the story to bump one of the not-so-famous guys from the story—I had a guy I wanted to add. Then I called up the stubborn anchorman and asked him if he'd like to be included.

I can still recall the moment I did it and how squeaky my voice sounded because I was unbelievably nervous. But there were two things I knew for sure: one, that he'd say yes, because what guy wouldn't want to be hailed as one of the bachelors of the year, and two, he'd feel obligated to take me out for a drink.

And that is how I met my husband.

How to Be Too Big for Your Britches

It's one thing to have an appreciation for making a dress from velvet curtains, it's another to be able to come up with a scheme like that yourself. But you can do it. It calls for only two things.

First, you have to have gumption. Personally, I think most women have gumption, but they simply aren't using it. According to my dictionary, gumption is actually a combination of *courage* and *energy*. The courage part means that you must have the guts to take chances, be daring, and not always do as you're told. You have to be willing to say, "I'm going to think about things in a different way. I'm open to looking at a pair of curtains and seeing a dress."

This is only mental bungee jumping, so there's no danger of cracking your skull. Still, it may be a big leap for you, especially if you have a tendency to follow the rules, to accept what people say as the way it should be. A few years ago I stopped by to visit a friend who had just gotten her first apartment in New York. She'd made lots of new purchases, including four large floor pillows, the kind you flop around on when you're watching TV or talking with friends. When I saw the pillows I burst out laughing. Each one of those very attractive pillows, made with fabulous

African fabrics, was still sporting an ugly tag that said "Do not remove under penalty of law." Now, even though each tag had a little qualifier—"except by consumer"—she had obeyed the order. Because the tag said so. To get what you want, you have to be willing to ignore the tags that say "Do not remove."

And then there's the energy part of gumption. You have to have enough initiative to get out of your chair and tear those curtains down. Too often women wait for things to come to them, for fate to make the first move.

Deborah Feingold, a top photographer in New York and someone we use frequently for *Redbook,* told me once that for years she yearned to find a good man, but she had no luck until she listened to the advice of a male friend who told her, "You know, you're going to have to work as hard on this as your career." That remark was a wake-up call. "Up until that point I had been sitting around, waiting for it to happen," she says. "But he was right. I was going to have to use some energy and creativity. I was going to have to do things, join things."

Feingold and a friend cooked up an idea, not unlike mine. They went to a magazine and proposed a photo story on single firemen (as far as she was concerned, firemen were cute and nice). They visited fire stations around New York, and the chief would get on the P.A. system and ask all the single men to come down for a casting call. When Feingold saw this one guy, she knew he'd be perfect for the story— and she says she knew instantly that she would marry him. And that's exactly what happened. The two even rode in a fire truck to their wedding reception at the Waldorf-Astoria.

Second, you have to be very clever. It's not just a matter of being willing to look for dresses in curtains, you must be clever enough to see them there. It calls for ingenuity and imagination. Fortunately, it's not as intimidating as it sounds. Part of being awfully clever is simply deciding that's what you're going to be and setting your mind to it. I have a friend named Bobbi Howell who is a senior vice-president of an advertising agency, and she lives by the principle that there is a clever solution to everything—she just has to find it. When she and her husband decided they wanted to move from Texas to Manhattan but she didn't want to leave her job behind, she convinced her clients that they'd be far better served working with the New York office of the advertising agency. Last summer after she learned that the day camp she was trying to enroll her daughter in was completely filled, I asked her what she was going to do. "I'm thinking about starting a scholarship for an underprivileged kid," she said. "Then maybe they'll make room."

Start with Bobbi's point of view. Now you simply have to *find* the idea. Here are eleven strategies.

11 Ways to Come Up with Smart, Clever, Bold, and Wicked Ways to Get What You Want

1. *Make what I call the kitchen sink list.* Write down every possible approach you can think of that will lead you to your goal.

If you have a friend who you trust and is always affirming of your efforts, brainstorm with her. Brainstorming is not only fun and freeing, but the other person or persons just may have the information and insight you lack. For instance, let's say that what you want more than anything is to go to Europe for the first time, but you can't quite swing it financially. You're trying to come up with ways to get there cheap. Your own list might include lots of good ideas, but not that great tidbit your friend happens to have stumbled on in a travel magazine: that in parts of Italy you can get free room and board in many old houses by helping to restore them.

Once you have your list, spend a few minutes thinking about each strategy, even those you may be tempted to reject as moronic. Pretend that this is the strategy you *must* use. How would it work? How could you pull it off?

2. *Chill.* Get away from the effort altogether. Go for a walk, listen to music all afternoon, read magazines, take an audio tour through the museum, ride your bike. When you take your mind off the subject this way, you not only give your subconscious a chance to percolate but you fill the well with ideas to draw from.

3. *Look up.* Or across the room. Or out the window. Sometimes we get so close to things that we don't notice that just outside our range of vision is something we can work with.

Designer Kate Spade says that she gets ideas for her fabulous handbags by people watching. "I'll see this old guy wearing a jacket and tie," she says, "and think, 'Oh my god, that tie could be the most amazing lining for a bag.'"

4. *Take a little success and make it bigger.* Sometimes you can be sitting on some little victory that could be blown out and put to much better use. When Ivana Trump was running the Plaza Hotel, she wanted to create as much buzz and excitement about the hotel as possible. One of her great ideas, which generated tons of press, was to accept reservations for people to eat at a little table in the kitchen of the Edwardian Room. I did it once and it was one of the most fun evenings I'd ever had eating out. My husband and I sat at this tiny table as the cooks and waiters dashed about. As we ate we watched all the food being tossed and seared and flambéed—it was like being in the middle of an off-Broadway play. "It made us a fortune," Ivana told me recently. "People were willing to pay the highest prices to eat there."

Where did the idea come from? Ivana didn't just think it up one day. Rather, it sprang from something small she was doing. She often visited the kitchen and ate there at a little table the kitchen staff set up for her. She enjoyed it so much she eventually had some of her friends join her. And if it was that popular with them, why not go big with it.

At *Redbook,* one of my goals was to develop a smart new health column that would be just right for our audience of young married women. We had a health page—called, surprise, surprise, "Your Health"—of five or six short items on everything from preventing a cold to feeling less pain during a mammogram, but it was kind of ho-hum.

We bounced around all sorts of ideas but none seemed right. One day I asked someone to take the reader ratings on all the health items from the past two years and rank them from high to low. A fascinating pattern emerged. The most popular items were all ob/gyn stuff. There was obviously a super urgency among women to be informed about issues like fertility and pregnancy and breast cancer, more so than about colds and flu and planter's warts. We took one look at that information and decided to create a column called "Ob/Gyn."

5. *Pretend you're Madonna.* When you're trying to generate an idea or an approach that's bold and memorable, it sometimes helps to experiment being someone else. If Madonna were going after it, what would *she* do? How about Sharon Stone? Or Hillary Clinton? Or Diane Sawyer?

6. *Hijack a great idea.* In certain cases the most creative thing you can do is recognize how someone else is pulling off a victory and then just copy them. Actress Jill Hennessy, who for three years played an assistant prosecutor on "Law and Order," says that when she first started on the show, as the only female lead, she felt boxed out and didn't know what to do. "Each week," she reveals, "the actors would get together for a meeting with some of the writers and producers and talk about the script. I was a twenty-four-year-old girl when I started and everyone else in the room seemed to be over forty-five. I would offer a comment about the script and no one would blink an eye. Or I would simply be silent because I just didn't know what to do. After the meetings were over, I would go home and cry. I thought, 'I've got to find a way to be heard.'"

The strategy that ended up making all the difference for her was one she simply stole from the men at the table.

"I decided to sink to their level. I mimicked the way the

men talked to each other. They weren't afraid to make eye contact. They didn't watch their words as much as women often do, and so there was less hesitancy when they spoke. And there was a certain tone to their voice, a gravity. I copied it all, made eye contact. I'd say things like, 'I totally disagree with you, man.' And I spoke loud enough. When you get the volume, you get attention."

7. *Hijack a great idea, part 2.* You can copy a strategy from someone who is successful doing what you hope to do. But there are other tricks worth stealing from completely different arenas. That's what I did when I got one of my first jobs as editor and had to negotiate a salary package. I was extremely nervous about negotiating for myself. Not only did I have zip experience, but I'd be meeting with two corporate-type guys who were masters at it.

Coincidentally, my husband had recently finished negotiating his employment contract, though in his business, TV, an agent does it for you. I envied him. How nice to have someone else do all that asking and bargaining. Then a little lightbulb went off. If it worked in my husband's field, maybe I could make it work in mine.

I called up my accountant, Harry, and begged him to come with me and play the role of my quasi-agent. He said yes only because he didn't know what he was getting into.

I will never forget that day. We met in this wood-paneled corporate office, the two top guys, me, and my accountant, who began to sweat as soon as we walked into the room. I had explained to the guys in suits that I wanted my accountant present in case there were money issues that I didn't understand and they were agreeable, though as soon

121

as they saw him they gave him a look that told me they thought he was totally bush league. We started with a review of the contract and the financial plan that was being offered to me. Harry got confused in a couple of places, simply due to nervousness, and I could tell by the expressions on the other guys' faces that they were convinced he was an amateur. Once I even saw them exchange glances, as if to say, "Who is this bozo?"

When we were finished going over their proposed plan, the suits suggested that they give us a few minutes alone to review everything privately. About fifteen minutes later they tapped on the door, entered, and asked, "Are you done reviewing?"

Harry glanced up and announced, "Yes, we're finished. And now we're ready to negotiate."

Their heads snapped back in surprise. And over the next half hour Harry began hammering away, getting me more and more money. Years later one of the two bosses told me, "That guy really did you good."

8. *Find the back door.* With most goals in life, there's one fairly obvious approach that presents itself immediately. And we often spend a lot of time trying that approach, varying it slightly if it doesn't work the first time. But it's often smarter to can that strategy and begin again. Think about the ultimate goal for a moment. Is there a way to get the exact same result by going down a different road or in a different door. That's what I did with the anchorman who became my husband. My friend suggested that he call me. When that didn't work we brainstormed and she tried to prod him through a variety of techniques, including laying some photos of me in front of him. What I finally focused on was the goal: I needed to meet him. And I came up with a totally different way to do that.

9. *Ask yourself what would happen if you did the exact opposite of what they're expecting.* Sometimes it's hard to abandon an obvious strategy because it's tried and true. It's worked brilliantly in the past—even for you—so who are you to question it? But it doesn't hurt to take a look at that kind of approach and determine whether it just might be a little tired—or perhaps in this particular situation, you could dazzle everyone by doing just the opposite. Earlier in the book I mentioned a trial lawyer named Suzelle Smith. Several years ago, Smith tried a case on behalf of a family whose twenty-six-year-old daughter was abducted from a shopping mall and then raped and murdered. Smith, who was suing the mall, decided to use a bold not-the-way-it's-usually-done strategy that made the whole jury connect with her. Usually, in these kinds of cases, the victim's family sits at the table with the attorney, a show of solidarity. But Smith asked the family to sit in the public seats of the courtroom. She felt that if she sat all alone by herself at the table, the jury would identify her with the slain woman. She was victorious—to the tune of $12 million.

10. *Remove the restrictions and see what happens.* Often, your creativity is limited or you feel stuck because you've bumped up against a set of rules. Sometimes they're official rules, or they may be rules people have simply made up and passed along. If you want to work at a particular company, for instance, people may tell you that you have to *know* somebody. When I was trying to figure out ways

to see more of my new son after my maternity leave was over, I mentioned to a stay-at-home mom that I was considering changing around his schedule so that he didn't go to bed until about 10:00 P.M. instead of 7:30. "That's not good," she told me. "Babies need to go to bed early." *Who says?* What I've discovered is that women who get what they want thumb their noses whenever somebody tells them "You have to . . ."

One of my favorite stories about a woman who ignored the rules involves Christiane Amanpour, the highly respected foreign correspondent covering the Middle East for CNN. Several years ago, when her contract was up, there was plenty of speculation that she would leave CNN, where she'd worked for years, and go to one of the networks. And that made perfect sense on one level. She'd become a star, so why shouldn't she capitalize on that to get a megabucks deal—plus wider exposure—on a bigger playing field? On the other hand, CNN still offered lots of appeal. An all-news channel gave her more airtime than she'd have on a network, plus she felt loyal to the place that had fostered her success. As she wrestled with her decision, I'm sure people she knew were offering lots of "shoulds."

Well, the fabulous thing about Amanpour is that in the end she didn't choose. She got *both*. She worked out a deal that enabled her to report for CNN *and* for CBS's "60 Minutes."

There's a great little trick a very wise woman once taught me about how to turn around a rule and think more creatively. First, you simply write down the basic rule everybody seems to be constantly repeating to you as if they were brainwashing you in a closet like Patty Hearst. In the case of Christiane Amanpour, she probably was told over and over again, "You're going to have to decide between CNN and one of the big networks." Then write down a second phrase, one that simply negates the first. In the case of Amanpour it would have been, "When your contract is up, you *don't* have to choose between CNN and one of the big networks."

Then let yourself go. Allow the second phrase to be your jumping-off point for some fresh, bold ideas that never occurred to you when you were locked into the "rule." In Amanpour's case, stating she didn't have to choose would have triggered lots of creative ideas. "Okay, I don't have to pick one or the other. What does that mean? That I can have both? How would I do that?"

You might have to play with a few sentences to get it right. A few months ago I used this approach and ended up with this tiny but fantastic triumph in my personal life. It's so silly, but it illustrates the concept beautifully. I was asked to give a speech in San Francisco and decided to take along my son, Hunter, because I thought he would love the city, most of all Alcatraz. Being a nine-year-old male, he loves bad guys, police, danger, intrigue, and all that stuff. As the week of the trip approached, I felt pretty relaxed because I'd planned everything carefully, including getting us a great hotel with a wonderful view of the city. But when I called two nights in advance of our departure to order tickets for the boat to Alcatraz, I was told snippily that they were *all sold out*—for my entire stay. Thanks, it seems, to the movie *The Rock,* Alcatraz was enjoying renewed popularity and you needed to book a week in advance.

Well, I almost started balling my eyes out in my office. Alcatraz was practically the whole reason for the trip— and there was no way I could resign myself to not going. So first, I tried the wear-my-heart-on-my-sleeve approach with the woman in ticket reservations. I talked about my son, how much the trip meant, and basically begged her to help. She sounded about as concerned as you'd expect her to be if I'd just announced that my cuticles were too dry. Next, I resorted to bribery. I asked to be switched over to the p.r. director and flung my editor in chief title around, even hinting at a story in the magazine. If I thought it would have helped, I would have promised a coverline (can you just see it?—"The Amazing Escape Every Woman Should Know About"). The answer was no, no, no. The boat could only hold so many people. I actually sat at my desk and wondered if I could possibly swim to the island like a dolphin with Hunter on my back.

Two days later, on the plane trip to San Francisco, I tried to keep Hunter from seeing how miserable I felt, but it was tough. Plus, I was getting a cold from all the Alcatraz stress. As I stared at the Airphone in front of my seat, I suddenly felt a rush of adrenaline, and I began trying that little trick my friend taught me. "You can't go to Alcatraz." "You *can* go to Alcatraz." That sounded nice, but it didn't do me any good. "To go to Alcatraz you must have tickets from that nasty boat line—and there aren't any left." "To go to Alcatraz you *don't need* tickets from that nasty boat line."

Suddenly I began to wonder. Was that boat line really the only way of getting there? Could there be another option?

I called my assistant from the plane, and asked her to start calling around to see if there was another way to get to the island. Maybe there were private tours or a helicopter service (I'd pay anything!). When I rang her back later, she had great news. One of the calls she'd made was to Greyline Bus Tours, because she knew I'd already arranged to take a Greyline trip to Muir Woods. It turned out they offered a three-hour city tour, at the end of which they dropped you at Fisherman's Wharf and handed you a ticket for the Alcatraz boat—and there were two spots open. By doing it this way the two tickets to Alcatraz were going to cost me $60, but I couldn't have cared less.

11. *Go for the burn.* You think you've finally got a nice new approach or idea. Well, don't stop there, keep working with it. Remember the early Jane Fonda workout tapes and how she taunted you to "feel the burn." Well, you have to do just that when you're planning your strategy. You have to keep pushing. Maybe you can take the idea even further.

Though designer Kate Spade does lots of fantastic handbags, she is perhaps most famous for her signature bags—the ones with the simple black-and-white label bearing her name on the outside of each and every bag. If you've seen the bags, you've probably assumed that these labels were a brilliant marketing strategy on her part. But they were actually a last-minute idea, a refusal on the part of Spade to leave well enough alone.

"Early on in the business, I was planning to include these simple nylon bags in the line," says Spade. "One night a friend of mine and I were getting the final ones ready and when we were finished I looked at them and said, 'There's nothing for your eye to go to.' But at the same time I don't believe in hardware and I don't like a lot of those little things you see on bags. And then I thought of something and it was the label that was inside the bag. I loved the look of the label, especially the typeface. By the way, Kate Spade wasn't my name then—it was the company name, a combination of my first name and the last name of my partner, Andy Spade [to whom she was engaged and later married]. So the label was just a design to me. I could have bought it at a trimming shop. We sewed them on the outside by hand and our thumbs were swollen at the end."

When It's Time to Break the Law

Being playful, toying with new concepts, getting funky— all of these things will help you find the plan B or Z that you need. Sometimes, though, you may have to go further. Sometimes you may have to break the law.

I'm not suggesting that you drive eighty-five miles an hour or write bad checks all over town. What I'm saying is that there are times when in order to get your way you may have to ignore a rule, or an order, or a sign that says DO NOT PARK or DO NOT DISTURB or DO NOT GO BEYOND THIS POINT. My friend Nancy Glass, the former anchor of

"American Journal," told me a great story of how she was a naughty girl to get a story.

She'd been sent to the airport by her executive producer to get an interview with the secretary-general of the United Nations, who would be arriving shortly from overseas and at the time was involved in some headline-grabbing story. When Glass and her crew arrived at the gate, they discovered that they were the only press there. Good. There wouldn't be any problem securing a brief interview. But before long, more and more reporters and crews began to materialize, and airport security felt compelled to stretch one of those yellow "police line–do not cross" tapes between the press and where the secretary-general would be walking.

Though Glass was in the front of the pack, she knew the tape was going to prevent her from pulling off the interview. So she took out her Swiss Army knife, sliced the tape down the middle, and proceeded to hold on to the two pieces so that no one could tell it had been cut. When the secretary-general walked by, she dropped the two pieces of tape, stepped forward, and put the mike in his face, bagging the interview she'd come for.

It's a risky business, breaking the law. Always ask yourself these questions first:

- What's the worst that can happen if I get caught?
- Will I end up with some short-term victory but long-term disadvantage?
- Will I anger anyone who is an ally?

- Will I enrage someone I might need to turn to for assistance someday?
- Will I wake up a day later ashamed to leave the house without a baseball cap on?

2 Things to Always Keep in Mind

1. Just because it's never been done before doesn't mean you can't do it.
2. Just because someone says you shouldn't doesn't mean you can't.

6

NEVER MIND YOUR OWN BUSINESS

If you've been following the advice I've offered so far on getting what you want, you've discovered that it's an ongoing process. It would be nice if all you had to do was make your pitch to *one* person or pull *one* fresh trick out of your hat but, unfortunately, it practically never happens that way. You ask someone for something you want badly and they send you on to someone else. Or they just out and out say no. You make a presentation that you're sure will knock their socks to the other side of the room, and it falls flat. Or they tell you it's close but not quite right. Or it turns out they weren't really the right people to be talking to anyway.

When that happens, you must simply regroup. You need to rethink your strategy. Or you need to take your glorious passion and dazzling ideas to someone else. The trick is to understand that getting what you want will often involve some rejiggering—of your ideas and your plans and your list of the right people to call. In order to rejigger effectively and keep moving in the right direction, you need a constant flow of information and a constant influx of names of people who can help. The only sure way to get these things is to ignore a piece of advice you've been given over and over again: Mind your own business.

Remember the first time someone snapped this phrase at you? Perhaps it was one of your parents. You'd just walked in on a heated discussion they were having about Uncle Bob's affair with the woman in accounts receivable and you blurted out, "Is Uncle Bob in some kind of trouble?" Or maybe it was a kid at school. You'd summoned your courage to walk over to a group of other fifth-graders congregating in a circle and inquired, "What are you talking about?" The nasty reply from at least one of them? "M.Y.O.B."

Regardless of who said it to you, it stung—and each time you heard it after that, it probably reinforced the idea that the wisest course of action in most circumstances was to keep your mouth shut and your butt out.

But women who get what they want know that they have to butt in. They talk to everyone they can, gathering tips, strategies, and names that will help them. Effective butting in also means working with their eyes and ears—looking and listening for essential information.

Of course, the right method is essential. If you go about it in a brash, boorish way, you will end up with nothing. People may not tell you to mind your own business as they did when you were eleven, but they will send you off to Siberia in whatever way they can.

Be a Snoop

One of the best ways to butt in is to take a deep breath, keep your mouth shut, and look around you. Much of the time we're so overwhelmed with our own needs or our nervousness in a situation that we are unable to observe what's really going on. You need to be a snoop. I don't mean you should be looking through anyone's wallet or medicine chest, but you have to keep your eyes peeled for info that can help you. Here's how:

• *Show up early.* No matter what you're after, when you must go someplace as part of the process, it really can help to get there early—before the pack or before everything begins to rev up, *especially* if you don't have a clue as to what to do. Getting there early allows you to see the lay of the land, to have a chance to relax before everything starts, to talk to people you might not have a chance to chat with later, when everything gets crazy.

After Donna Hanover was chosen for the part of Ruth Carter Stapleton in Milos Forman's *The People vs. Larry Flynt,* she made a point of showing up on the set a day ahead of schedule. Though she'd had bit parts in movies before, they were always as a local anchorwoman. This was her first real role.

"I got there early enough so that I could watch Milos Forman direct some scenes the night before," she says. "I can go into a situation and evaluate it pretty quickly, but I know that I need to keep my eyes open for a while before I open my mouth. And that's what I had a chance to do— to watch him give instructions and watch how he interacted with the technical people and to find out who on that crew would be friendly faces for me the next day, who would be able to give me feedback, who would want me to succeed."

• *Watch how people sit*—and stand and move their arms and touch their faces and interact with one another. People who know something you need to know but aren't going to tell you often give it away in their body language, in the way they move around the room. A friend of mine who's a consultant told me a fascinating story about how noting people's body language had saved her a huge chunk of money. "I'd been working with this company on an idea I'd developed and they seemed very excited about the project," she says. "We didn't have a signed contract but they'd agreed to the concept verbally with some modifications, which we were in the process of working out. There'd been three follow-up meetings, and though things were moving at a sluggish speed, they were definitely moving, and I had no reason to be worried. Then we had our fourth meeting, and it felt very weird to me. Their lips were moving the right way, and everything they said indicated they were okay with the project, but—and I know this is going to sound strange—they seemed to be sitting very stiffly in their chairs. At first I tried to ignore it, but later, at home, I forced myself to accept that it might be an indication of a problem. I started making a contingency plan for myself. I arranged a quick lunch with someone who had also expressed interest in the project. I set some balls in motion. And sure enough, the other people pulled out three weeks later because their company was being sold. The people at the meeting knew it was happening, but they'd been told not to tell anyone and to go through the motions with people they were doing business with. I was furious, of course. But at least I'd listened to my instincts about all those stiff backs at the meeting. I got a head start on taking the idea to someone else. If I'd waited three weeks, it would have been too late to make it happen with the other company."

• *Listen between the lines.* People often tell you what they want you to know in indirect ways, without framing the info as important, and you should pay attention every time you catch yourself saying, "I wonder why he said that?"

I work with a young editor whom guys adore, and she is so good at picking up cues. She told me a story lately about how she dealt with an issue her new boyfriend had. "One of the things that Dan talked about on our first date was the fact that his ex-girlfriend was so unreasonable and jealous of his being at work all the time. I have taken that to heart and run with it. For example: One night he got stuck at work and we kept having to move our dinner plans further back and further back. When he finally got to my apartment, he looked like a puppy that was waiting for his punishment. Instead of getting upset, I took his side and said, 'I know how upsetting it must have been getting stuck in a meeting when I know you would rather have been here with me. Let's get your mind off of work right away and go have a great evening.' He was so relieved to be praised rather than punished that now he makes twice the effort to plan ahead with his boss when we have early evening plans."

• *Connect the dots.* Fabulous snooping isn't simply a matter of spotting something and realizing that it's worth knowing. It's filing away information for future use, as well as recognizing that what you spotted makes even more sense when you connect it back to something you saw the day before—or the month before.

Why You Should Talk to Absolutely Everyone

As Donna Hanover says, sometimes you keep your mouth shut and your eyes open. But that approach will give you only so much information. Next you must talk—not just to people who can obviously help you but to those who are simply in the same room with you or on the same plane. Strike up conversations wherever you go. You must do this even if you feel tongue-tied and would much prefer to be nursing your drink. These people may have information you need or they can point you in the direction of people who do.

After Donna Hanover got a look at how Milos Foreman interacted with his crew, she went right up to some of the friendlier faces. "I introduced myself," she says. "I knew the next day that some of them would be rooting for me. And the next day some of them did help me. They'd say,

'Try this . . . try speaking a little louder' or 'Turn your head to the right.' "

When we interviewed Fran Drescher for *Redbook,* she revealed that her big break had resulted from striking up a conversation on an airplane. In 1992, she cashed in some mileage to fly first class to Paris, and she just happened to sit next to the then president of CBS entertainment. At this point Drescher had lots of movie credits and a leading role on the short-lived CBS sitcom "Princesses," but she was hardly a household name. She made a beeline for the bathroom to put on some makeup and then came back and pitched him the idea of a show that would play off her personality. By the end of the flight, he was intrigued—and in less than a year, "The Nanny" had become a reality.

Do you absolutely dread this sort of schmoozing? It may be because you're not exactly sure what to say or you assume that the weird look on people's faces is annoyance. Generally it's not—they're simply as uncomfortable as you are. Try these four little strategies.

1. Stick out your hand and introduce or reintroduce yourself.
2. Ask "How did you get involved?" or "How do you know Pamela?" or "What brought you here?" They will love telling you.
3. If you're in a totally unfamiliar setting and the person seems friendly, admit that you're new or an outsider. They may be inspired to help.
4. If you've struck up a conversation and you see someone hanging awkwardly on the side, bring him into the

conversation ("We were just talking about . . ."). He'll be grateful for being rescued (and everyone else will marvel at your graciousness).

The Perfect Way to Talk to People

Did I just write a section advising you to talk to everyone? Let me actually rephrase that slightly. I don't believe you should simply *talk* to everyone. I believe you should *sweet-talk* them. Yes, in the late nineties I'm advising that you should be a sweet-talker, no matter how much that runs against the grain of what you've heard. That's the strategy used by women who get what they want.

All through the eighties, women were encouraged to talk tough. We were supposed to ask for things brusquely, show we meant business, cut to the chase, keep it impersonal, bark when we didn't get our way. It made sense on one level, I suppose, because it gave us the appearance of not being total pushovers. In the short term, in many instances, it probably worked. We made people sit up and pay attention. And yet when you think about how human beings operate and what they like and need, how could we possibly believe it made sense in the long-term? No one likes to be barked at or bossed around. Oh, yes, sometimes you may have to resort to it—when you've tried nicely and they're not behaving—but always start with sweet talk.

I can still recall the moment all this jelled for me. It was a number of years ago, while I was working as editor in chief at another magazine, and I was on a business trip with the publisher, a fabulous woman a few years older than I was. We were being screwed by the airline somehow—I don't even recall how—and as we stood at the counter getting the bad news, I was readying myself to launch into my hear-me-roar-and-rant-and-rave-tough-girl mode. But suddenly the publisher opened her mouth and, in the most honeyed voice, said something like, "Harry [she had read his name tag], we are so exhausted from our trip that we can't even think straight. We desperately need your help. What would you suggest is the best thing for us to do?"

He rescued us somehow, though I don't remember exactly how—I believe we got bumped to first class—but whatever happened, it was like magic. I finally recognized the truth that day: You really can catch more flies with honey than with vinegar.

Since that plane ride I've had a heightened sensitivity to this art, and I've paid attention to the women who are masters at it. The woman who apparently wrote the book on it is Elizabeth Dole. When she was the keynote speaker at a *Redbook* luncheon in Washington, she was unbelievably charismatic and dynamic and personable. She asked people about themselves, hung on their every word, and never appeared to be bored with what anyone was saying. Of course, that's the public persona. How is she behind the scenes? Well, guess what nickname she was given during her two stints as a cabinet member because she was so masterful at getting her way? "Sugar Lips."

It's time to put on your sugar lips, and though you may not end up sitting on two presidential cabinets, I guarantee those sugar lips will get you far. Here's a brief guide to the art of sweet talk.

- Be devastatingly charming.
- Be charming because you really mean it. You can't just stand there doing it with greed in your heart. You have to learn to enjoy the connection with other people, the pleasure of making someone feel good that day.
- Be charming to *everyone*. Don't play favorites. Don't be a giant ass kisser to the rich and powerful and ignore everyone else. Charm must be egalitarian. Donna Hanover says that whatever station she worked at, she always befriended the people who worked with her behind the scenes. "In dealing with the people who really taught me my job, the cameramen and the editors, I found that if I treated them with the respect they deserved they would look out for me and give me story ideas. They were really the engine that got the newscast on the air, anyway. There was one cameraman with whom I got to be friends while I was anchoring the news in New York City. We were covering a big Brink's robbery up in Hartford, Connecticut. Seven million dollars had been stolen. We covered the press conference and then we were driving around the town trying to find some kind of information about the suspect: Where did he live, where did he go to school, where did he shop? There was no way to figure it out; we didn't know Hartford very well. We're driving down the street, and all of a sudden, he pulls up short and says, 'Go into that gas station and ask if they ever met the guy.' And I said, 'Nat,

what are you talking about?' And he said, 'Just do it.' And I did. And sure enough they had. Well, Nat had seen three Brink's trucks lined up on a side street next to the gas station, and detective-cum-longtime-cameraman that he was, he'd thought, Maybe that's where they service the trucks and these people may have met him. Cameramen and editors have shown me how to deal with lighting and have come up with a key question that makes an interview that much more incisive."

• Ask them about themselves. It's old advice, but always worth repeating.

• Flatter them, yes, but better yet, ask their opinion. I think telling people they look great or that they have wonderful ideas is fine, but if you don't really believe what you're saying, it will sound awful not only to them but to you. A much better way of connecting with people is to ask them what they think of something. They'll enjoy telling you, and their opinion may just prove to be valuable. Lisa Caputo, former press secretary to Hillary Rodham Clinton, told me that President Clinton will ask twenty people working in the White House what they think of something. I'm sure he's doing it to get a broad spectrum of opinion, but you can be sure everyone loves telling him what they think.

• When you must come right out and ask someone for a name or a tip or a piece of advice, be up front about needing it—and cast the other person in the role of "mini-mentor." Say: "You've been so terrific to give me all this information. It's going to be a big help to me. Is there one particular person you would suggest I call?"

How to Work a Room

Over the years I've seen a few women work a room beautifully, but one of the best is businesswoman Janet Atkins. She says she learned from several women she met when she was in her twenties who took her under their wing. Here's her strategy: "You walk into the room and size up who's there and who you need to talk to," she says. "If you only know the person who invited you, ask her to introduce you to her four favorite people in the room. Try not to monopolize anyone too long. When you move on, hand out a business card, which you should carry in your left-hand pocket, not your purse, so that it's easy to reach.

"What do you say to people? If you know someone important is going to be there, and you hope to make an impression, do some research first and ask their opinion on something going on in the industry. They love that. They always think, 'Great, she thinks I'm an expert.' If you can't think of anything specific to ask, a favorite question of mine is 'Tell me about the best conversation you had this week.' If you get stuck with a bore, tell him, 'I must introduce you to someone fantastic.' "

How to Find Out Something Bad You Need to Know

The kind of butting in we've been talking about is, by and large, the pleasant kind. You're meeting new people, getting in touch, trying out those sugar lips. But there's another kind of butting in that isn't pleasant, yet is sometimes necessary. On some occasions, you may have to go searching for information about yourself that's not so nice to hear.

Let's say you're not making progress with your efforts. You've been turned down or left dangling or you can't even wedge your foot in the door. You're not sure why, and yet you know someone who is in a position to have access to the information because of his or her job or location. If you approach that person the right way, there's a chance he'll tell you what you need to know.

First, before I tell you a trick that will get someone to cough up ugly truths, you have to ask yourself if you really, really want the news. Sure, knowledge is power, but it can also make you miserable—or worse, paralyzed. Once you know what others are thinking or planning, it may cast a big shadow over you and not allow you to make decisions based purely on what your intuition or experience is telling you.

If you give it lots of thought and decide that knowing is best, here's the advice of a very successful friend of mine who gets everyone to tell her everything. Once, when she was in danger of being ousted from her job for political reasons, she got so much information from the players close to the person in power that she was able to use it to maneuver effectively and protect herself.

She says never pressure people into telling you lots of specific information. The idea of having to give up gory details about, for instance, why you were passed over for membership in the tennis and swim club will make them uncomfortable and they're likely to say nothing at all rather than spill those kinds of beans. All you may need to know anyway are the broad outlines. So, let them play multiple choice. For instance, say, "Was it a matter of not having lived in the area long enough or was there someone actually opposed to my membership?"

Once they give up the info, my friend warns, *do not react*. Simply listen, nod, and say, "Thanks for letting me know." Do not scream "I can't believe it" or "That pig, I should have known" or "They've got a helluva lot of nerve." This will not only shut down the flow of facts, but it will also discourage that person from ever telling you anything again. She'll be afraid that in your lunatic state you'll do something with the info that will come back to haunt her.

How to Listen for What You Really Need to Know

So far I've been focusing on what you should say to get the facts you need. But another big component of gathering essential details is *listening* to what people have to say. We've heard over and over again how important it is to be a good listener, but even when we mean well, we do poorly at it. The women who get what they want know how to listen very, very well.

There are whole books written about being a good listener, but there are three tips that I think will serve you perfectly and allow you to skip the books. My tips all come from women who have made a success of listening very carefully to other people.

1. *Do your homework.* If you want to hear anything good, juicy, or useful, you must start with the right questions. Martha Frankel, one celebrity profiler who gets movie stars to say the most amazing things, told me she spends the days before an interview reading every single article about the person that she can get her hands on and watching all of his or her movies on video. And, she says, it's always worth the effort.

"You can read sixty articles about someone and they'll all be the same, but in the sixty-first you'll find *one thing* that's different and worth asking about," she says. "I did a piece on Rob Lowe a little while ago. Every article had these variations on the girls and drugs and alcohol problems. It was endless. And then, buried deep in one of the last articles I read, there was a comment he had made about how he feels hostility radiating from the people he meets. I was totally intrigued by that. This guy has a nice, amiable face, and I wondered why people would be hostile toward him. When I met him in L.A. I didn't bring it up right away, but later I asked him, 'How do people react to you?' He said people are usually really hostile. It's ironic, but the story he told about that really said more about him than anything else."

Sometimes you just can't turn over a whole weekend to research, but you can always do your own Cliffs notes version. Read the top sheet, ask anyone in the know for a capsulized version of the person's background. They say a little bit of knowledge is dangerous, but in a case like this, I think something is always better than nothing. When I was on the publicity tour for my first book, one of the discoveries I made from talking to publicists and other authors was that TV and radio interviewers rarely have the time to read the book before the interview. At least in TV there's a producer to put some decent questions together, but radio hosts generally just wing it—and in some cases it really shows. Along the way, someone told me about a female talk-show host in Texas who did super-sounding interviews because she took five minutes to study the table of contents. She'd say things like, "Ted, I know from your book that there are five big mistakes first-time investors always make. Let's talk about them."

2. *Form as many of your questions as possible from what the person just said* rather than from what is bouncing around in your head. I once heard former *Washington Post* writer and novelist Sally Quinn talk about interviewing and she said one of the smartest things you can do is to let go of your preoccupation with your next question and listen closely to what the person has just said. Far too often, someone will unload a fascinating tidbit, but because we're so busy anticipating what we're going to ask next, we don't hear it.

3. *When the person has finished answering a question, don't say anything.* If you can resist rushing in with your next question or comment, the person may fill the vacuum by elaborating on what she just said or revealing an unexpected truth. It is hard to do at first, and you may feel like each minute you wait is an hour, but keep trying—it really works. I learned this from one of the most brilliant writers around, a guy who has produced provocative profiles of celebrities and newsmakers for all the top magazines, including *Vanity Fair.* I confessed to him several years ago that I felt my interviewing skills left something to be desired and asked if there were any guidelines he could share. He told me about this strategy and claimed that it had worked fabulously for him. I know I said earlier that all my great listening tricks had come from women, and this one actually did, too. You see, the writer admitted to me that he had picked up this strategy from Helen Gurley Brown, or rather a woman who had worked for Ms. Brown and had told him how the *Cosmo* editor did this when she listened to people.

How to Not Look Like a Buttinsky or a Brownnoser

Though I've been singing the praises of butting in and sucking up, let's face it, there is nothing as obnoxious as someone who is obviously doing it. I still recall this writer who did it to me really blatantly when I was working as a senior editor in magazines. I'd met her at a press event, had a nice conversation with her, and later got together with her for lunch. Then she started calling me from time to time for favors. But that's not the part I minded. What bothered me is that whenever she called she'd spend the first ten minutes asking me all about myself and letting me go on ad nauseam until she would suddenly sound slightly distracted and then drop the bomb—her need for a favor. I'd realize that she had only let me run on at the mouth because she needed something and wanted to get me in the right mood. I fell for it on more than one occasion because she always sounded so sincere. Afterward I'd feel used and embarrassed for having talked her ear off about a boyfriend who said he'd call back but didn't or some dental work I was dreading.

To avoid appearing like the Contact from Hell:

- Be up front about the favor stuff. Start the call off with "I'm calling to ask a favor" or "I could really use your help." Then after you've gotten that out of the way you can ask how the person is doing.
- Read the signs. Do they seem less than eager to talk to you, slightly uncomfortable when you're talking? Time to back off.
- Always, always write a thank-you note to someone who has given you information or advice—even if it wasn't worth much.
- Whenever possible, find a way to give the person credit.
- If at all possible, make them glad they did it. A colleague of mine recently described a friend of hers who can get anyone to do anything. In the summer, when the woman in question goes jogging, she convinces various people to pick her up in their car so she doesn't have to jog back—she hates going over the same ground twice.

    "How does she get them to do it?" I asked.

    "She always takes you out to breakfast afterward and she's just so much fun to be with."

7

KEEP YOUR ELBOWS ON THE TABLE

top for just a moment. Before you begin reading this chapter, I feel I should flash one of those statements they use at the start of "NYPD Blue" that claims you may find some of the material offensive. No, you're not about to see any frontal nudity, but what I'm going to say might be offputting. I'm going to suggest that in order to get what you want you sometimes have to do things that you've been told in the past aren't things nice women do.

First, a story. A year or so ago Ted Koppel devoted one night of "Nightline" to opera, in conjunction with a special event at the Kennedy Center, and one of his guests was an eightysomething-year-old woman named Kray Vayne who in her prime had been considered one of the great opera singers of her time. And yet despite her extraordinary voice she achieved only a modest level of success. "I went forward," she said, "but I never hit the jackpot. I was always on the periphery because I didn't belong to any company."

Why didn't she achieve the fame she deserved? An opera critic on the show offered this explanation: "In order to make a career in any of the performing arts," he said, "you've got to have elbows. It's not enough to have talent. You have to have the ability to put yourself out there, to put yourself in front, and, quite evidently, she was lacking in the last of these qualities."

It's pretty sad to think that a remarkable singer didn't get the attention she deserved simply because she refused to elbow her way to the center of the room. And yet that's a fact of life. In some situations you will be given what you want because your passion bowled them over or your ingenious idea won the day, but there are times when you absolutely have to be a little pushy. If you want to be the one chosen, you have to be noticed—and noticed for the right things.

Consider what a male reporter said not long ago about Barbara Walters: "I always think back to the time when, as a reporter, she used to beat out the assembled male press corps, elbowing her way to the front of the pack and driving her high heels into the feet of her colleagues." She wasn't afraid to use her elbows when necessary.

Here are ten strategies that will help you get what you want. They're not *required,* so if you feel uncomfortable about trying them, ignore this chapter. But if you've got the nerve, they can give you that extra little something that helps you secure what you're after.

1. Be a Show-off

We've all heard from the time we were young that it's not nice to be a show-off and yet if you want to get noticed by the right people, you must strut your stuff.

It's not quite as hard—or as repulsive—as it sounds. A big part of being a good show-off is simply showing up—at places where you'll see and talk to people who can help you.

In *Redbook* we used to have a page called "My Favorite Things" that featured paparazzi shots of celebrities wearing some of the latest fashion trends. Each month I had to go over lots of these photos with the art director and narrow them down to a group of eight or nine. Most of the photos were taken at movie premieres and there would be shots not only of the actors in the film but also of hot celebs who were invited in order to make the opening a star-studded event worthy of press attention. Well, one day I realized that during a stretch of about eight months, I'd looked at what seemed like a billion shots of Sharon Stone in a billion different fabulous outfits. It finally occurred to me what she was doing. She didn't have a movie of her own during this period, so she was locking down her superstardom by going to *other* people's openings—and she probably upstaged all the other actors at most of these events. The pièce de résistance was her outfit for the movie premiere of *101 Dalmatians*. It was black and white and furry and was just *cuter* than what Glenn Close, the star of the movie, was wearing that night.

151

You don't have to go everywhere, but you should go places where your presence will remind the people who matter that you're definitely in the mix. And don't *just* show up. Wear something fantastic (buy a couple of show-off suits or dresses to wear to these occasions) and introduce or reintroduce yourself to anyone in a position to change your destiny.

2. Be a Blabbermouth

One of the smartest women I know in p.r. told me one day that it was essential to have a "big mouth list." At first I thought she meant a list of all the people you should never tell anything to because they'll blab it all over. But it turns out it's actually a list of all the people who should hear about your latest projects or triumphs—because they'll be sure to spread the word. The list should include bosses and former bosses, clients and former clients, contacts, anyone in your fan club, your hometown newspaper, your alumni magazine, people who have interviewed you, and so on. And there's a way to do it without sounding like the world's biggest braggart. To a former boss you could simply write, "Abby: I thought you'd get a kick out of seeing this because you knew me when."

Your big mouth list shouldn't be used solely for tooting your own horn. You should, of course, congratulate people on their accomplishments. Another great thing to do is to send them clippings that relate to something going on in their lives. Let's say a former client used to mention how his dream was to scuba dive off the coast of Sri Lanka. You spot an article on the subject in *Travel and Leisure*. Rip and send. People love to be remembered this way. To make it easier to do, don't bother with a note. Always keep a pad of Post-its on your desk (use the same color consistently so people will come to associate it with you) and scrawl a fast "Just in case you didn't see this" across the top.

3. Be Slick

You've read those stories about how celebrities get "packaged." One minute she's just an ordinary girl from Ohio and the next minute she's got big hair, unforgettable lips, boot-cut pants that show off her belly button, and she's turning up in Liz Smith—all thanks to the magic of some agent or publicist. Though packaging has a kind of nasty connotation, it works because people absolutely do judge on appearances, and if you don't accept that you're being naive. If boot-cut pants are going to work for you, go ahead and wear them.

Ideas and projects need slick packaging, too. You have to make them appear hot, sexy, in demand, wanted in every state. That's what Nancy Taylor Rosenberg told me she did when she set out to try to find an agent for her first book.

"When I finished the manuscript for *Mitigating Circumstances,* the next step was to figure out how to get it published," she says. "I bought a book that listed all the agents and also told how to write a query letter. I thought, I'm *never* going to hear back doing it that way. My husband had been in marketing and sales and he told me, 'You have to package yourself,' and so I decided to do that.

"First I did a chapter-by-chapter outline. I put asterisks by three or four of the most dramatic chapters and then included those chapters in their entirety. This way an agent would have a chance to quickly understand the plot and read a sample of the prose without having to read the whole thing. I included a photo of myself and a bio—I thought people would be interested in knowing that I'd spent fourteen years in the criminal justice system.

"Then I decided to get a little devious. People in my writing class at U.C.L.A. had critiqued the book and said a lot of good things about it. So I made a page that said, 'Praise for *Mitigating Circumstances*,' just like you see on the back of a book jacket. I quoted most people verbatim, though I did pump up some of the weaker quotes. Under each name I added the name of the book they'd been working on in class—*Joe Blow Goes to New York* or whatever. No one would have any way of knowing these books were unpublished manuscripts."

Though she got tons of rejections, one agent bit—and the book sold to a publishing house for $787,000.

4. Make Something Sound Better Than It Is

Packaging is taking something you know is good and giving it sex appeal so that you attract someone's attention. But sometimes you have to go a step further—you have to take a slightly negative thing and make it seem positive.

Makeup artist Bobbi Brown, who has enhanced the faces of many, many celebrities and models, launched her own terrific line of makeup and skin care products in 1990, called Bobbi Brown Essentials. Brown told me that at the time she could only afford to do a limited number of products, and thus her introductory line included only ten lipsticks. What Brown did was make the limited number seem like a brilliant concept. She called her cosmetics "an expertly edited range of essential products." Her press release stated: "The line will never include hundreds of shade options as there just aren't that many shades that women look good in. Instead, color has been simplified by confining shades to those that are truly beautiful and wearable." Having just ten lipsticks suddenly sounded like a perfect idea.

5. Cut in Line

Cutting in line is rude behavior. And for the most part, I recommend against it. Not only do you develop a bad rep, but your karma is bad, too. But sometimes what looks like a line *isn't* a line, and you're silly to conform. I went to a White House conference for editors recently, and all the early arrivals took seats around a big conference table where a variety of cabinet members would be speaking. When a group of us who had been on a delayed flight showed up, we automatically skulked over to a row of chairs along the wall, even though there was an empty place at the table. But one especially ballsy editor ignored the penalty chairs and took the one empty seat at the front of the table. When Madeleine Albright came in, she sat right next to her. The editor had ignored the supposed "line" the rest of us were so stupidly conscious of.

6. Act Like You Know More Than You Do

I said earlier in the book that I'm a big believer in plunging in, taking the bull by the horns. You want to be prepared, but it's far better to jump in and learn as you go than to sit around waiting until you're perfectly ready. The downside of this approach is that once in a while you get caught not knowing what you should. Personally, I absolutely believe that, where possible, you should fake it rather than reveal your ignorance. Here are a few strategies.

• If you have time, quickly accelerate your learning curve by getting other people to give you the information you need. Don't admit your stupidity. Tell them you'd like their thoughts and evaluations.

• See if you can buy yourself some real time. Simply say in a friendly, brisk, and efficient manner, "That's a good point, let me get back to you on that right after this meeting." Or say, "I have some thoughts on that and I'd love to put them in writing for you."

• Get *them* talking. When I was being interviewed for the editor in chief job of *Child* magazine, the president of the company asked my opinion of a rival parenting publication—and much to my horror I'd never heard of it. Now,

I'd done tons of homework for the interview, combing through every issue of *Child* and talking to lots of parents, but since the field was new to me, and I was only recently a mother, this particular publication had just never come across my radar screen. In one split second, I had to decide whether to wing it or confess my ignorance—and look like I was seriously uninformed. This guy was a super businessman and I knew he'd hold it against me if I said "Gosh, I've never seen that one." So I looked him straight in the eye and said, "I like some things they're doing, but overall the magazine doesn't excite me. How much of a threat do you think they are?"

He launched into his opinion, and fortunately never asked me any more about mine. I got the job!

Janet Atkins, former vice president of external affairs at the University of Virginia's Darden Business School, endorses this approach wholeheartedly. "If you're stuck, definitely try redirecting it. I think it works 99 percent of the time. Besides, they probably want to tell you what they think anyway."

7. Tell a White Lie

It's one thing to exaggerate slightly in the name of packaging or to act like you know more than you do. There may be occasions, though, when you consider going further and telling a little white lie.

Bobbi Brown found that a harmless little white lie worked for her after the buyers at a major department store who had verbally agreed to sell her first lipsticks changed their minds. "I was overjoyed when the store told me they would take the lipsticks and then practically the next minute they were calling to say they couldn't—the buyer said she checked and realized they had no room," says Brown. "The next day I was doing the makeup for an ad for another store and someone in advertising expressed interest in my products, saying that perhaps *that* store would carry the lipsticks. I called back the buyer at the first store and said that I just wanted to let her know that another store was now interested. It wasn't a real lie, but it was definitely a stretch because the person I'd talked to had only been in the advertising department. Well, the buyer said, 'Let me get back to you.' And then she called back to say she'd definitely carry the lipsticks. The store obviously got nervous at the idea that someone else might get it and they wouldn't."

I have a friend who told a delicious white lie to make sure that the interior renovation on her home was completed on schedule: "I'd heard over and over again from friends that contractors and workmen are notoriously bad about deadlines," she says, "and I couldn't stand the thought of the project going on for months. So I told a lie. I said that my sister was getting married in my home on a certain date and that everything had to be done by then. Within the workers' earshot, I'd pretend to talk on the phone to florists and caterers and even my sister, to whom I loudly swore that 'the dear men are working so hard— they wouldn't do anything to spoil your important day.' The work was done several days ahead of schedule."

158

Of course, when you tell a harmless little white lie there is always the danger you will get caught and look silly or treacherous. Right after Sandra Bullock became a major star in *Speed,* there were articles about her everywhere and many of them mentioned that in high school she had been voted Girl Most Likely to Brighten Your Day. It was such a fabulous detail because it seemed to indicate that she was destined to be adored. But a few years later, a reporter doing research for a profile of her discovered that she had not actually won that title. It had gone to Barrie Britton. Sandra Bullock, however, hadn't come away empty-handed. She had been voted Class Clown and Funniest, a two-time winner—but, of course, neither of those titles has anywhere near the adorableness of the other, nor do they have the date-with-destiny spin.

It may not have been a deliberate deception—if it was, it seems a pretty harmless white lie (though I can picture Barrie Britton forced to send for her high school yearbook to prove that it was *she* who had produced all that sunshine). There's just the embarrassment of being caught at doing something that runs against the grain of who people think you are.

8. Value Style Over Substance

Having spied for years on the women who get their way, I really believe that appearance counts, and you should pull out all the stops, every day—whether you're going for a job interview or trying to convince your child's teacher to give her more attention. In my experience it's always better to be overdressed than underdressed. People just give you more respect. And what's really fabulous is to create a signature look for yourself, one that people always associate with you. Someone pointed out to me recently that model/actress Elizabeth Hurley has one of the most distinctive fashion looks around. It seems like she has zillions of outfits, all of them different, but if you look closely, all her suits and dresses have the same line—they're formfitting and nipped in at the waist. She's always in heels and she wears no jewelry, except a diamond crucifix.

9. Be an Ambulance Chaser

The term *ambulance chaser* generally refers to a personal injury lawyer who shows up at the scene of an accident and tries to sign up the bloodied and battered passengers, with a promise to help them get a megasettlement from some insurance company. Loosely it means anyone on the prowl for opportunity, especially the kind that pokes out of the heap of someone else's disaster. When I suggest that you be an ambulance chaser, I'm using the term in a more benign way. You've got to be on the lookout for great possibilities and not be afraid to give chase. A friend of mine confided in me recently that there was a job she was dying to have and she heard that the woman who had it was not performing as hoped. My friend knew the top person from a previous job situation and asked her to lunch "just to catch up." During the lunch she never once mentioned the specific job or anything about the other woman. But when that job opened up, my friend got the call—and she swears it was because she'd made sure she was on the top person's mind.

Another great ambulance chasing story: I was invited once to this fabulous apartment of a woman I was going to be dealing with on a project. I complimented her on the place, and she whispered, "I heard the people who owned it were getting divorced and I jumped before anyone else could."

Look for opportunity everywhere—even in disaster.

10. Be Bitchy When It's Really Necessary

I believe that if you can avoid it, it's always better not to be bitchy. And it's not simply because the world is a better place if you're not. Even if you get initial results, these days people don't tolerate bitchiness for long and in many cases it absolutely won't make anyone jump. That's because so many people today don't feel ownership for what's at hand, and so your bitchiness just doesn't scare them. Try chewing out the customer service representative for the mail-order catalog that screwed up delivery of the wedding gift you sent someone. She just doesn't care that you're threatening to take your future business elsewhere because it won't have any impact on her personally. You're much better off trying to use your sugar lips and walk away with a 25 percent discount on your next purchase.

Before you resort to bitchiness, I suggest a round of hardball. You act tough, make your demand, hint at the possible consequences, and hope you scare the other person into giving you your way. The hitch to hardball, as a p.r. whiz I know says, is that you have to be ready to "take your toys and go home"—because there's always a chance the other person won't budge.

But sometimes, yes sometimes, bitchiness—yelling, huffing, throwing a hissy-fit—is necessary and it gets results with people who are not giving you the attention, respect, or effort you deserve. There are three things I always want to be sure of if I'm about to be a bitch:

1. That graciousness definitely wouldn't work better.
2. That bitchiness will have the power to motivate the person and get me what I need.
3. That being bitchy won't backfire on me.

I always try to keep bitchiness short and straightforward (no curse words under your breath). Think of it as a test of the emergency broadcast system. It doesn't have to last long, but it should be unmistakable that there's a problem and you are vastly unhappy.

The last time I was truly bitchy was at the Ritz Hotel in Boston. My flight was delayed and when I arrived at the hotel at 11:00 P.M. the woman at the front desk announced, without any apology, that they were overbooked. I'd be staying at another hotel across the river, she informed me, and the fact that I had a reservation didn't matter. Not only was I ragged and in need of a bed immediately, but some-one was picking me up at 5:30 A.M. in front of the Ritz to take me to a radio station where I had to do a broadcast, and now I would have to get up even earlier to get across the river and back to the Ritz to catch my ride. I told her it was unacceptable and asked for the manager. I screamed. I was a total bitch. Ten minutes later I had a suite with a fireplace.

8

DON'T SIT TIGHT

I'm about to reveal one of the world's best strategies for meeting men. It was given to me when I was single by a woman who had more suitors than she knew what to do with, and by following her suggestion I was introduced to dozens of very eligible guys, many of whom I ended up dating. If what you want is to meet a guy, I swear this tip will help—but I'm actually passing it along to make a totally different point.

As I mentioned earlier, after I got divorced in my early thirties, I discovered that meeting men in New York City was a challenge. Yes, friends were willing to fix me up with their male acquaintances, which was an okay method, but eventually most people I knew had coughed up the one or two guys they considered appropriate, and I had hit a plateau.

I summoned my nerve to ask advice from a woman I was

just beginning to get to know. She lived in a beautiful apartment on Park Avenue and had a kind and successful husband. I knew from mutual friends that she'd had a legendary social life during the years before she'd met her husband.

"My dating life is in the doldrums," I told her. "How do I meet some decent guys?"

"Oh come on, you're doing fine," she said.

"I've had my good periods," I told her. "But I'm in a dry spell right now and there's no end in sight. Give me some advice."

"Well, there *is* one thing that worked really well for me," she said, "something someone else taught *me*. You have to entertain."

"Entertain?" I said. "You mean *sexually*?"

"Nooo. I mean you need to give dinner parties and cocktail parties and just entertain."

"I don't get it," I said. "How does that help you to meet guys? Do I ask people to bring guys *with* them?"

"No, no, just entertain. You'll see."

So that's what I decided to do. I was mostly convinced that nothing would come of it—after all, if I threw a party for my friends I'd have no one there but couples, gay guys, and girlfriends. Where were the single dudes supposed to materialize from? But I was game to give anything she suggested a try.

Cocktail parties done right—no jug wine or bags of Cheez Doodles—were out of my budget, so I decided I would become known for casual dinner parties on Sunday nights. My cooking skills were barely above adequate, and

I had a tiny, tiny kitchen with literally two feet of counter space, so I bought lots of cookbooks, particularly those that emphasized uncomplicated dishes made more appealing because they were presented on beautiful platters. I had hits and I had misses. One night I prepared a shrimp dish in some kind of roux sauce of butter, milk, and flour and I made an error with the timing or stirring. The sauce turned into a kind of plaster so that the shrimp were served in little body casts. And I still recall this one night when I was trying to lift this huge hot roasting pan of twelve Cornish game hens out of the oven and I didn't have any place to set it and the heat was starting to burn through the mitts, and all I could think was, "This is *really* for the birds."

Did I meet any guys? No, not a single one—at least not right away. I gave countless dinner parties and although once someone actually brought along a cute mystery guy, and he asked me out twice, that was all that ever materialized at these soirees. But over time a funny thing happened. The people I entertained began entertaining me in return. I was invited to dinners and parties and barbecues. Over the next year I met tons of guys. Several chapters ago I told the story of how a friend of mine "found" my husband for me on her first day at work. I think she had me on the brain in part because I'd included her in three dinner parties in a row after she'd moved back to New York.

As I said, if you're having no luck meeting men, try this trick. It really does work like magic. But I bring it up because it's also a parable. What was confirmed for me by all my baking and braising and sautéing is that motion begets motion. To get what you want you must keep moving, generating action and new opportunities. If you sit tight, nothing will happen.

This is certainly true when you hit a plateau or face a setback. But it is just as true when everything is going your way. Actress Jill Hennessy says that several years ago someone arranged for her to have lunch with director George Lucas, and he gave her this advice: "Always work, just work. Maybe it's not the right time or right character, but if you're too fussy, you might lose out." He had given this advice to Harrison Ford.

What to Do When Things Are Stinky

You've tried the ideas in the book and unfortunately you seem to be spinning your wheels or you've been out and out rejected. Let me take you through some emergency strategies.

When They're Leaving You Hanging

One of the most annoying things that can occur when you go after something is to be ignored by the people you've called or written. They're in a position to grant you your wish or give you access to what you need, and though they know you're waiting, they've apparently decided to let you park in limbo for a while—and they may even be enjoying the thought of you stuck between heaven and hell (or at least that's the way it seems). Though this is an unscientific opinion, I'm convinced this limbo stuff happens more and more these days. Your four options:

1. Give it a few more days. There's an excellent chance that their lack of response has nothing to do with you or your idea and relates only to the fact that they're crazed. There have been so many times in my work life as an editor when someone—a writer or celebrity, for instance—calls with a "yes" after leaving us dangling for weeks. I sit there and wonder why, if they wanted it, did they jeopardize the situation by taking so long to respond. Often it's because life got in the way. TV anchor Nancy Glass told me that when she's feeling anxious about someone not getting back to her, she reminds herself of something Paul McCartney said when she interviewed him. She asked him, "What do you think about when you sing 'Yesterday'?" His reply: "What I'm having for dinner that night." As Glass says, "When you present an idea to someone and you don't hear back, you assume that all they've been focusing on is your idea and why it's pathetic, but what they've really been doing is thinking about dinner."

It also doesn't hurt to play a little hard to get. Wait a day or two before starting to nudge.

2. Now, try nudging. Don't sound annoyed. Tell the answering machine or the secretary that you'd appreciate it if you could hear back by such and such a date.

3. Ask yourself, "Have I made myself or my idea as compelling and irresistible as possible?" Maybe you haven't heard because they're busy, but it could also be that they *sort of* like your idea but they're just not *wild* about it. There's an interesting phenomenon I've noticed over the many years I've been reading assigned and unassigned manuscripts that come in from writers. Because editors in the articles department are so busy with the day-to-day stuff of editing pieces and getting them through production, they tend to let incoming manuscripts pile up. By the time a manuscript goes from the articles editor to the executive editor to me, it may have been kicking around the office for several weeks, and there's sometimes even a pleading note from the editor on the top sheet saying, "Rush, please. Sorry I sat on this." And then I may sit on it a bit longer.

When the editor calls the writer back to talk over the revision or announce why we may be flat-out rejecting the piece, she'll apologize for the delay and explain that everyone was swamped and the piece just took forever to circulate.

But here's the interesting phenomenon: The really great pieces never take very long to circulate. Somehow they always rise to the top of each editor's pile and then shoot down the hallway like a bullet. And that's because when the editor first gets a manuscript in, she doesn't just stick it at the bottom of her pile of things to read. Instead, no matter how crazed she is, she sneaks a peak at the first paragraph—if it's really juicy and compelling, she *keeps going*. She is suckered into reading the entire piece ahead of all the others in the pile.

This happened to me yesterday. I was just about to add a new manuscript to my batch of "to reads," and I glanced down at the opening paragraph:

"She vanished. Her disappearance seemed so astonishingly complete, impenetrably baffling for five agonizing weeks. All that she left behind on the front steps of her house were a can of grape soda and the class assignment that she had carried outside to study during that balmy autumn afternoon."

How could I possibly stop reading? I was hooked—and everything else went to the bottom of the pile.

If you haven't heard back there's a chance they're just busy, but there's also a chance you haven't captivated them. Whatever you suggested just hasn't knocked their socks off.

It may not be too late. You still have a chance to modify what you've presented. My entertainment editor is fabulous at doing this. Not long ago we put in a request to shoot a cover story on an actress who had recently broken up with her boyfriend and had been in two dud movies—back-to-back. Because she had a new movie coming out, we thought we had a good shot at a cover and the publicist was very encouraging. But after we made a formal offer, nothing happened. The entertainment editor gave it a few weeks, then nudged nicely. Still nothing. "You know what," she said, "they're not bowled over by our angle." She thought for a day and kept coming back to the fact that the publicist had said the actress was nervous about discussing the boyfriend and the bad movies and didn't want to focus on the past. So my editor pitched a new idea, a sort of day-in-the-life concept that would involve following the actress around for a few days. They said yes almost instantly.

If they're stalling and you don't know why, come right out and say "Can I get you more information?" or "How can I make this as appealing as possible to you?"

171

4. Move on. Sometimes being ignored by someone or listening to them hedge is a sign that they're busy. And sometimes it means you just haven't made them pant. But sometimes it can mean they have absolutely no interest in your lovely little concept—or *you*—and never will. So why don't they come right out and tell you rather than letting you sit around staring at the phone. Because some people are bozos and jerks and don't know how to say no or aren't gracious enough to do it well. Trust your gut. If you get the sense you're being given the runaround, go to the next best person on your list.

When They Flat-Out Say No

No is an awful word to hear. It can make you cry, scream, wail, be nasty to old ladies asking directions, drink four frozen margaritas, even sit in a stupor watching reruns of "Silk Stalkings." For some of us, it's hard to even get moving again when we hear a big no.

And yet there's something fascinating I've noticed about women who get what they want. Hearing the word *no* may annoy them, even bring a tear to their eye, but it doesn't leave them in a stupor or a heap on the floor. Instead it seems to galvanize them, energize them. I was sitting once with an extraordinarily dynamic woman when she got a phone call that ended up being a no on something that was important to her. Though she made a few faces at the phone for my benefit, she was perfectly gracious and allowed the other person to get off the phone fairly quickly. When she put down the receiver, I was half expecting her to yell the *F* word across the room, but she just looked down at the table with her hands in a fist against her mouth. And then she said with a burst of energy, "Okay, okay." It was as if she was saying, "*No* is bad. *No* stinks. But now I know where I stand and can go after it another way."

Women who get what they want don't see *no* as the end of the world. To them it's information and ammunition—and it's immensely better than being left wondering. Here are two ways to use *no* to your advantage.

1. Try again, using what you've just found out. Whenever you hear *no,* you must do everything in your power to find out the reason why. Sometimes they just won't tell you. And sometimes, like the boyfriend who splits saying "It's me, I'm just not ready yet," they give you some feeble excuse to make you feel better rather than be honest about why you're not lighting their fire. But sometimes they *do* tell—either voluntarily or because you've artfully pulled it out of them—and that information is extremely valuable. Say something nonthreatening, like "I appreciate your getting back to me. It would be very helpful to my future efforts if you could tell me why you chose another whatever."

If you have information that impacts on what they're saying, make another pitch. A friend of mine had just settled in at a new job when the person above her quit to go elsewhere. She would have been the natural choice to replace him—if all of this had transpired a year later. It just seemed like an awfully big job for the company to give someone who had only started a few months before. Happily for her, the head of her area felt she was worth the gamble and suggested she meet with the president of the company to make her pitch. They connected immediately— and yet the president seemed reluctant. My friend pushed to hear what he was thinking.

"Are you worried because I've been here only four months?" she asked.

"No, that's not a concern. I just think the actual job may be a stretch for you."

That's all she needed to know. That night she wrote a memo titled "Ten Reasons It's Not a Stretch to Give Me the Job."

A week later it was hers.

Unless you are absolutely convinced that they will despise you if they hear your voice again, go for it at least one more time.

2. Move on to person two or seven or one hundred— and know that you only need *one* person to say yes. There are many, many people with great ideas who have been rejected by absolutely everybody—except one. And it was that one acceptance that turned them into a thrilling success. It doesn't matter how many people have said no if you can find one who says yes—and you must simply keep searching for that one.

When we interviewed FBI special agent Sue Hillard for *Redbook,* she said something that beautifully sums up the need to let go and move on. Hillard is a top shot, one of only nineteen women in FBI history to make the Possible Club, an honorary fraternity for agents who shoot perfect scores on one of the toughest firearms courses in the country. Unlike some agents, she doesn't berate herself over missing a shot because that would only make her tense. "What helps me the most is remembering that once you shoot a bullet, it's gone," she says. "You can't bring it back, so you shouldn't be thinking about it. You should go on and shoot the next one, which is also a good philosophy of life."

Author Nancy Taylor Rosenberg approached dozens of literary agents before she found one who would take her book. She tells a great story about something that happened right after her book hit the jackpot.

"Not only did I sell *Mitigating Circumstances* to a publishing company, but I also sold the film rights to director Jonathan Demme. And in a matter of weeks, I even signed another contract for $3 million for four more books. But every day I went to my mailbox and found a stack of rejections from agents to whom I'd sent the book ages ago. 'We cannot sell your novel,' they said on their mimeographed forms. The news about my book and movie deal was in all the trades—*Publishers Weekly, Variety,* the *Wall Street Journal,* the *New York Times*—but still these fools were rejecting me. Boy, did I get a kick out of that. Well, I guess you can safely say they never read the book, but I also guarantee some of these people are still kicking themselves in the pants as they kissed off a great deal of money. So this is to say don't get discouraged. I was rejected by almost every agent in the United States. All it takes is one."

When You Don't Like What They Say

Sometimes you hear back and the answer isn't a no, but nonetheless it's not an answer you like. Keep looking.

175

That's what twenty-four-year-old Denise Oppenheimer of San Francisco did. Just before she was due to start law school in San Diego, she experienced pain and watering in one eye. She went to an eye doctor, who then directed her to UCLA's renowned eye clinic for tests. The diagnosis: She had choroidal ciliary melanoma—a malignant tumor of the eye. And their recommendation: Her eye had to be removed immediately.

Denise and her family were horrified. Rather than take the doctor's recommendation, they kept turning over other stones. Her sisters spent two nights on the Internet, looking up everything they could on eye tumors. Her grandmother asked her doctor for advice. Her mother called a referral organization called Best Doctors in America. One name kept turning up: Dr. Jerry Shields in Philadelphia. Denise flew to see him and learned about a risky procedure he does in such cases. She decided to go ahead with it. He removed her tumor surgically without removing the eye—and followed up with radiation. She has her eye today.

"If they hadn't questioned and researched and asked," says Denise, "I know I would have lost my eye."

What to Do When Everything's Going Your Way

Fantastic! You got what you wanted, what you'd always hoped for, and now it's yours to savor. But keep in mind that the "Don't Sit Tight" rule applies as much to the times when you get what you want as to the times when you don't. It's essential that you not only take care of any unfinished business and thank anyone who helped, but you also must do whatever you can to build on your success. You're probably thinking, "Jeez, don't I even have ten minutes to enjoy my prize?" By all means, rest on your laurels (see Chapter 9), because if you can't enjoy your success, why go after it? But you also want to protect your winnings.

• Write thank-you notes to absolutely everybody who helped. Thank-you notes are, of course, something you do because you're a grateful, appreciative person who recognizes that someone really went to bat for you and that it made a difference. But there's another reason you must do it: People get really weird if you don't. Over the years I've been repeatedly struck by how bent out of shape someone will become if they have not been properly thanked. And yes, I've turned weird myself. I once went out of my way to help get an acquaintance's girlfriend interviews with several top people in my company. I never heard a word from her until the day I saw her in the lobby of my building. She said she had been hired by one of the people with whom I had set her up. I was so miffed I could barely talk to her when I bumped into her again. Often the annoyance or anger someone feels about not receiving the proper gratitude strikes me as disproportionate to the offense, and yet the point is that they feel it and their resentment can come back to bite you in the butt. A friend of mine confessed to me lately that she had helped a friend's wife get a contract for a project through her company and that the woman had never called or written to say thank you. Later, when the

177

project hit some rough spots, she was in a position to help but did nothing. "Her ideas were basically good," she says, "and I was being small not to help, but I was so annoyed that she'd never thanked me. It immobilized me."

Protect yourself from the wrath of the gods and write that note. Even if you put it off and are now tortured because you didn't do it and think it's too late, go ahead. They may not even notice that three weeks have gone by—and it's better to be late than not to do it at all.

• Make them think they're brilliant for picking you or saying yes to you. In many situations a thank-you note or call is all the closure you need. If, for instance, your cousin has nicely arranged for you to meet a couple in the town where you just bought a house, a note is probably enough. If the couple is sensational, maybe you also want to invite her for a barbecue once you've unpacked your grill and scoured the grime off.

However, whenever you're going to have ongoing inter-actions with the person doing the giving, let them see that they were very smart to say yes to you. Maybe it's a reward—or a great confirmation of their ability to pick a winner.

A friend of mine who is in charge of soliciting major gifts for a university says that once they get a big-dollar gift from a donor, they make the giver feel like a million dollars for giving. They host a reception in his or her honor. They put up a plaque. They arrange for the person to meet anyone who will directly benefit from the gift.

If you have finally gotten your husband to help out with the kids' baths in the evening, you absolutely must make him feel good about it—even though your reaction is, "Oh, puleeze, it's about time he lifted a finger." Let him see right away that the direct result of his effort is a happier you in the evenings, who has time to serve the two of you cappuccino after the kids have gone to bed. This will prevent recidivism on his part and lay the foundation for the next request from you.

With new bosses or leaders (in volunteer work, for instance), it's essential to convince them that you've hit the ground running, even though you'd like a few weeks to get up to speed.

I used to be bad about doing this. I'd get in a new situation and pour my heart into whatever I was doing, but I'd never get up from my pile of work to let the right person know just how lucky she was to have someone like me at the other end of the hall.

When I was hired in my late twenties to be the executive editor in charge of articles at *Mademoiselle* magazine, the editor in chief who hired me took a risk. Though I'd been editing lots of articles in my previous position, it had been four years since I'd been at a women's magazine, and I was rusty when it came to topics like "Will He Call Again? Four Ways to Tell Before You Kill Yourself." The first few days on the job, I parked myself in my office, reading piles of articles, trying to get a feel for the types of pieces that were assigned and which writers could do what. Well, in the middle of all this, my boss began calling me every few hours to inquire how I was coming along on ordering business cards. The first time she called I thought it was slightly odd for her to be so concerned with trivial matters, but perhaps she was trying to be helpful. By the third inquiry, I wondered if I was working for a madwoman. In hindsight, I realize she was nervous and probably wondering what I was *doing* down there. The business cards were her excuse to see what was going on.

What I should have done was arrange a meeting with her on day two and said, "I'm so excited about all the opportunities here, but first I need you to tell me what your priorities are. What do you think is missing? What can I do to make you feel we have the perfect mix of articles?"

And it wouldn't have hurt to ask her to join me at lunch with one of the great new writers I was planning to introduce in the magazine.

Ideally, those things would have made her think, Wasn't I clever to hire this girl.

• Figure out the *next* thing you must be an expert at and do it. To get what you wanted, you may have had to learn how to do something extremely well. Let's say your goal was to get into business school and you pulled it off. Chances are you read books, even possibly took courses on how to outsmart the GMATs. Nice work—but don't stop there. Once you've used your skill to your advantage, determine the next skill you need. You must create a new learning curve for yourself and master the next challenge.

In fact, Janet Atkins, formerly of Darden Business School, says that the women who excel at Darden recognize that getting in is only the first hurdle. "You can't just say 'I'm bright, I got in,'" says Atkins. "You have to arrive and acquire an understanding of the landscape, the politics, the interpersonal dynamics, how teamwork is done well.

You must network, find out who the powerbrokers are and emulate them."

One of the biggest complaints book authors share with me is that their publishing house did a crummy job publicizing their book. They say things to me like "They got me on some shows but they were the wrong kinds of shows" or "It turned out they don't do book tours for books like mine" or "The publicist they gave me was fourteen years old and she didn't know what she was doing." What is painfully clear is that once authors find out all they need to know about how to get a book published, their learning curve ends. As soon as the acceptance check was in their hands they should have been trying to find out the publicity plans, sizing up the strengths and limitations of the p.r. department, and exploring strategies used successfully by authors of similar books.

Once you achieve anything, pat yourself on the back for five seconds, and then figure out the next thing you must be an expert at.

• Be a Barbie marketer. The day I walked into the Gap and saw Gap Barbie on display, the strangest sensation came over me. Not only did I think it was a fabulous marketing move, but I wanted one for myself! Can't you just imagine what it's like at a planning meeting at Mattel Barbie. There's nothing Barbie can't do in their opinion, no place she shouldn't be. You have to learn to think like they do. You've got a good thing going—now what else can you do with it?

Christy Ferer is a reporter who has covered fashion and home for the "Today" show and is also the author of the fabulous little book *How to Decorate on a Dime.* She is also a successful businesswoman, and she told me she doesn't do anything without asking herself, "What's the *end* use of this?" In other words, how far can she take it, what other lives might it have?

Years ago she decided she wanted to come up with a way to let her weekend guests know what there was to do in New York City without having to go through a spiel each and every time. So she made a fun video in which she described the famous sites, and she got a few famous New Yorkers to talk on the tape as well. When it was all finished, it was perfect for her guests, but then she asked herself, "What's the end use?" There had to be something else. She approached one of the biggest hotel owners in New York and suggested he buy a similar version for hotel guests to check out on the TVs in their rooms. He took her up on it and today Ferer's company, Apple Vision, offers this arrangement for fifty-three New York hotels (she also runs Chicago Vision in forty Chicago hotels).

• Become a guru. Whatever win you pulled off, take advantage of opportunities to perpetuate the idea of yourself as the know-it-all in that area. Jennifer Kushell, president of Young Entrepreneurs Network, says she gets a kick out of the fact that *U.S. News* called her a "guru," and knows that there's no harm in perpetuating a label like that—in bios, in press releases, anyplace it will work.

9

REST ON YOUR LAURELS

It happened to me in the most clichéd way possible. My family and I had driven out to our weekend home not far from the Delaware River in Pennsylvania. As I unpacked the cooler in our little farmhouse kitchen, I noticed that our cleaning lady, who comes in for a few hours during the week while we're gone, had placed a tiny bouquet of buttercups in a Styrofoam cup on the counter. My heart did a little skip when I saw them. "How sweet of her to do that," I thought. "I wonder where they came from?" It wasn't until the next day that I realized they were blooming all over my own backyard.

Oh boy, I thought. It was a classic case of someone not taking the time to notice, let alone smell, the flowers. I knew all about how important it was to allow oneself such moments, but I'd become busy, crazed, preoccupied, fixated on what to have for dinner, when to shampoo the dog, and where to find cheaper panty hose. I hadn't realized how long it had been since I'd rolled around in the grass.

As I've watched and studied the women who get what they want, a particular truth has come into sharper focus in the last few years. It's one thing to have your cake and eat it, too. It's quite another to have your cake, eat it, and absolutely relish it.

Lots of things can get in the way of savoring your cake.

• You get what you want and though it's absolutely sweet at the time, you realize that now that all the work and effort are over, life seems anticlimactic.

• You reach your goal but immediately feel pressure to get on to the next one. (I heard Tipper Gore say in a meeting recently that as soon as you scale one mountain, you look up and there's another one staring you in the face.)

• Just as you're trying to enjoy your victory, there's a backlash or repercussions or a downside you weren't expecting. (After we moved into our supposed dream house, our baby-sitter told me she thought it was haunted, and sure enough, we would occasionally hear the sound of someone walking on the stairs when there was actually no one on the stairs. Great.)

• Sometimes, too, you can get snagged by that old impostor syndrome. They gave you all you wanted, but you come to suspect that they must have been idiots or were blinded by your charm.

If you want to be a cake lover rather than simply a cake eater, you have to allow yourself time to rest on your laurels. Here are nineteen ways I've seen it done:

1. *Savor, really savor, your accomplishment.* Pam Zarit, a wonderful speech coach with whom I've worked, told me that she received a postcard from someone that left a lasting impression on her. Not the photo but the message. It said: "Having a wonderful time; wish I was here." You've got to relish the here. Give yourself at least one day to be giddy about your success, to jump up and down, rub your hands together in glee, squeal in delight, and even snicker about those who claimed you'd never pull it off.

2. *Reward yourself beautifully.* When I was working at *Glamour,* a coworker walked in one day with the most gorgeous pair of diamond studs I'd ever seen. I noticed them from about forty feet away—they caught my eye like a hubcap in the sun—and I ran across the articles department to check them out. They were so white and bright and big. My first thought, of course, was that her boyfriend had proposed, but she confessed that she'd bought them herself. "I finished my book," she said, "so I went into Tiffany's and asked them to show me their one-carat studs."

Those diamonds still sparkle vividly in my mind and that's because of the reason she bought them. I'd never known a woman to reward herself for an accomplishment with such generosity. And the book in question was merely a short fitness guide that had taken six months to write. I can only imagine what she would have done for herself if she'd produced a history of the French and Indian War.

I've always tried to let those studs be a lesson. Great deeds deserve great rewards. It's particularly nice if the reward fits the deed. A friend of mine who recently lost fifty pounds treated herself to the most wonderful new clothes. She didn't simply buy smaller sizes. Her new clothes are all in fabulous fabrics like shantung, and great new colors like salmon and marigold.

3. *When someone congratulates you on your fabulous victory or coup, smile and simply say "Thank you."* Resist the urge to credit luck, to qualify the degree of success, or, God forbid, apologize for getting the goodies.

4. *Allow for buyer's remorse.* A friend of mine who is a successful real estate agent once told me that many new homeowners suffer from what's called buyer's remorse. They've plopped down thousands and thousands of dollars for a house they pursued with a vengeance, but not long after they move in they're overwhelmed by a sense of dread and anxiety and regret. It might be because the house doesn't seem all it was the first day they pulled up in front or perhaps it's turned into a money pit, but most often it's simply that the size of the commitment and responsibility is sinking in with terrifying force and magnifying the tiniest of disappointments.

A form of buyer's remorse occurs with lots of life's prizes (even with husbands). The trick is to ride out those feelings rather than try to immediately address them. Of course, if they're still nagging you in three months, it may be a sign that you need to reassess, but in the first months, do your best to ignore them.

5. *Consider the fringe benefits.* If you're suffering at all from a case of it's-not-as-good-as-I-hoped-it-would-be, take time to discover the hidden extras or advantages you might not notice at first glance. A friend of mine recently came back from a family vacation to France and Switzerland that she had spent months planning. It was her ten-year-old twins' maiden trip to Europe and the first time she and her husband had been abroad in almost a decade. For weeks before they left she'd barely been able to contain her excitement and anticipation—her kids were going to have the kind of adventure she'd never had as a child and her husband and she would be back in a romantic place they loved and sorely missed.

Well, it was clear by day two that her kids had about as much interest in European culture and history as they would have in a plate of snails, and they moaned constantly about all the walking and the sight-seeing. As for romance, my friend had planned to occasionally leave the kids at night with a sitter, but the twins were anxious about staying with strangers in a foreign country, so my friend and her husband spent far less time alone than they'd fantasized about. By day seven of a fourteen-day trip, she was starting to get a bad case of the blues. Then she realized something. All the time her family was spending bunched up together on trains and in hotel rooms was giving her a glimpse of her kids that she usually didn't see. She felt she was coming to know them better, to discover fascinating nuances. So she allowed herself to go with that and didn't dwell on the fact that they were missing the great museums. Her trip turned out to be a wonderful experience—but in a way she hadn't imagined.

6. *Rediscover your husband and friends.* If you've been working very very hard at a goal, you've probably been giving less than full attention to your support system. Of course, part of what makes them such a good support system is that they tolerate being ignored when you're under the gun. But now it's time to reconnect—and make sure that putting them on the back burner doesn't become a habit.

7. *Get rid of friends who refuse to let you enjoy your triumphs.* Not all friends are worth fully reconnecting with. There are some who are not only incapable of being happy for our success, but go so far as to seem downright miffed. You know the type I mean. You spend an entire winter toning your postbaby body and when you show up at a party in a sleeveless minidress, your friend says, "Aren't we getting a little old for the thigh-high look?"

I have several wonderful friends who make life's little victories even sweeter because of their supportiveness and their vicarious enjoyment of those victories. They're also there when things go bad—to console and add some perspective.

But I've also had a few friends over the years who could make me feel almost embarrassed when I felt happy, who could launch a zinger in my direction that had the power to nuke all the glory and excitement. Why have such a jerk as a friend? Well, it's never like that in the beginning. It's a problem that rears its head gradually, that you initially dismiss as a bad mood and then once you see it in full daylight, you're reluctant to throw an old friendship overboard.

When I was newly divorced, I got to be good friends with a work pal who was terrific about checking on how I was and making sure I hadn't fallen into some terrible slump. But over time I began to discover that if things *were* going my way, she could seem irritated or critical. I landed a new job, for instance, and she pointed out everything she hated about the new magazine. I started to think about cooling things with her, but I decided to give it more time, wondering if I might be too sensitive. One day I was chosen to run a panel on magazine publishing, and I asked her to be one of the panelists. In front of a roomful of editor wannabes, she acted dismissive of me and my comments. Afterward, someone I know who was in the audience took me aside and said, "I hope that woman isn't a friend of yours." After that she wasn't. And though it was awkward parting company, I never regretted taking her out of the picture. It was so nice not to have those little zingers coming at me unexpectedly.

If a friend can't share in your victory or, worse, makes you have second thoughts, it's time to move on.

8. *Draw your line in the sand.* If the prize you've won involves commitment on your part, you're going to have to rethink your schedule. Everyone talks about setting priorities, but I've noticed that women who get what they want have gone that extra step of writing them down—and sticking to them. They've decided what matters and what they will and will not do. Makeup artist Bobbi Brown says,

"My personal life always comes first." She takes her kids to school, she's home at a reasonable time, she works out of her home some days.

Think through what the commitment will take and what the best possible schedule would be and what you should say yes to and no to. And then be very, very firm—no one will ever protect your line in the sand but you.

9. *Don't let work expand to fill the allotted hours.* It's very easy to let a chunk of work take as long as you give yourself to do it. Whether it's cleaning the front closet or writing a killer memo, if you have one hour, it will take one hour; if you have two hours, it will take two hours.

Periodically resolve to leave the office thirty minutes earlier every night for a week and see if you can pull it off.

10. *Avoid always doing two things at once.* Doing more than one thing at a time has been a lifesaver for me. When I landed my first job as a magazine editor in chief, my son was just six months old, and I decided that the only way I was going to be able to leave the office at five was to squeeze in an extra hour or two of work somewhere else. A perfect place was during my morning and evening commute, but the New York City subway is so packed that there's practically no way you can leaf through papers or edit an article while you're hurling along. So I slashed my clothes budget and put aside money for a cheap car service. I was able to get an hour's worth of homework done during the daily rides—though many of the cars were really old and didn't have reading lights. I had to take my own flashlight during the winter months!

Over time, however, I realized I was taking the two-things-at-a-time strategy (sometimes three!) too far. I worked during "E.R.," leafed through catalogs while on the phone, mentally worked on *Redbook* coverlines during a massage. One day as I was headed down the East River in the car service, scribbling away on a legal pad, the smell of the river wafted in through the window and evoked a powerful memory of a day in Buenos Aires and a walk along the river there. From that day on I decided I would start spending part of the ride just leaning back against the seat, watching, listening, daydreaming.

11. *Write little notes to yourself.* With many goals comes not only commitment but pressure and stress. I know of several women who carry little notes to themselves in their wallet that they look at during the day when they're feeling pressured. The notes say things like "If it doesn't get done today, it'll get done tomorrow," "No one's paying me enough to panic," and "It's honestly going to be okay." Granted, it may sound a bit hokey, but they find that having such reminders keeps everything in perspective.

12. *Use a personal day to do something personal* (not stripping off old wallpaper, buying kids new shoes, etc.).

13. *Share the bounty with someone else.*

14. *Be a natural girl.* If you're finding that you've gotten just what you wanted, but the stress involved makes it hard to enjoy, get outdoors. Walk, look, smell, lie on your back and decide what shapes the clouds are making. Writer Wanda Urbanska says that moving to a small town helped her discover not only the pleasures of being in a natural environment but also how to summon those feelings elsewhere. "There's a wonderful nature trail on our property," she says. "I go there whenever I can and when I'm there I have this overwhelming sense of peace and honor. I've realized how important it is to take those feelings into my everyday life. I think many of us get away from experiencing plain old genuine feelings of happiness."

15. *Ignore your critics.* When you reach a goal it is more than likely that someone will find a way to criticize it or diminish it. I was introduced to some people recently at a dinner party, and when the host mentioned that I was the editor of *Redbook,* one of the women said, "I see that lying around the beauty parlor." It was as if she was saying, "It's nothing more than something women thumb through when they're letting hot air blow around their heads—and, of course, I've never bothered to read it myself." Now, I could have jumped to my defense but I've learned the value of advice I heard Helen Gurley Brown give a few years ago: "Don't bother answering your critics." Her point is that you have practically no chance of changing their minds, so why waste valuable psychic energy?

16. *Create an afterglow.* While there are some achievements you can ride for a long time, others are just a short hit and you can feel deflated after they're over. But there are ways to create an afterglow with some of those victories, to extend their life and their pleasure. It takes a bit of experimenting.

One of the things I wanted most in my twenties and thirties was to travel the world and, as I mentioned in the first chapter, a woman I know shared the secret with me. After I was divorced at thirty-one, I was earning enough that I could afford one really fantastic trip a year, and I put enormous energy into researching and planning the annual three-week journey. By the time the day of departure arrived, I'd be a ball of nerves and excitement. The trips were always full of the ups and downs you experience when you travel—occasional loneliness, long delays, the usual sort of things—but overall glorious and exhilarating. The problem was coming home. It was nice to climb in between my own sheets again, but I'd feel a wave of despondency because the adventure was over and there wasn't going to be another one for an entire year.

Then one year I had a revelation. I'd just returned from the island of Rarotonga, an exquisite paradise southwest of Tahiti in the Pacific Ocean (I'd been helping restore an archaeological site) and was as glum as could be as I headed out each morning for the subway. I realized suddenly that if I was having withdrawal problems, what I needed was another fix. So that night I walked over to the East Village and spent an hour in a sensory deprivation tank. Trust me, it's not for everyone, and I'm not sure I'd ever do it again, but when I left I felt fantastic. What I'd discovered was that when I returned from an adventure I needed to keep the adventure going in little ways.

17. *Carve out an itty-bitty space for yourself.* It's going to be hard to build on your success if you don't have a place to think and imagine, a nook or cranny where your muse is allowed but no one else. Find a corner to call your own— particularly at a special time each day. Use it to read, write, imagine.

18. *Know that you can take your act anywhere.* Women who get what they want may have once, for a moment, thought they were incredibly lucky, but they've managed to go beyond that line of thinking. They know they pulled off their victory because they worked at it. *And* they also know they can "do it" again—even in a different arena or under different circumstances. A very successful friend of mine told me that just after she'd gotten a divorce, several female colleagues took her out for a girls' night of commiserating and did nothing but moan about how bad things were out there. By the time she got home she was ready to sob. "But then I started thinking about myself in contrast with those women," she said. "I make things happen in life—across the board. So why should it be any different with dating."

Think about your skills as a toolbox that you can pull out anywhere. Instead of "The real estate market stinks, I'm never going to be able to sell my house," think "The real estate market stinks, but I'm a master at finding opportunities. What can I do to pull this off?"

19. *Sleep late.* Stretch out on cool sheets. Lounge in your jammies. Then get out of bed and plan how you're going to go after the next fabulous thing that you want.

ABOUT THE AUTHOR

Kate White is currently editor in chief of *Redbook*. After beginning her magazine career as an editorial assistant at *Glamour*, she moved up as a writer and editor at several national magazines, eventually becoming editor in chief of *Child*, *Working Woman*, and *McCall's*. She is also the author of the best-selling book, *Why Good Girls Don't Get Ahead . . . but Gutsy Girls Do.*